Spring Integration Essentials

Integrate the heterogeneous endpoints of
enterprise applications with Spring Integration
for effective communication

Chandan Pandey

open source*
community experience distilled

PACKT PUBLISHING

BIRMINGHAM - MUMBAI

Spring Integration Essentials

First published: February 2015

Production reference: 1160215

Published by Packt Publishing Ltd.
Livery Place
35 Livery Street
Birmingham B3 2PB, UK.

ISBN 978-1-78398-916-4

www.packtpub.com

Credits

Author
Chandan Pandey

Reviewers
Marten Deinum

Biju Kunjummen

Xinyu Liu

Luca Masini

Commissioning Editor
Julian Ursell

Acquisition Editor
Richard Brookes-Bland

Content Development Editors
Sharvari Tawde

Ritika Singh

Technical Editor
Aman Preet Singh

Copy Editors
Roshni Banerjee

Pranjali Chury

Project Coordinator
Judie Jose

Proofreaders
Ameesha Green

Joanna McMahon

Indexer
Monica Ajmera Mehta

Production Coordinator
Nilesh R. Mohite

Cover Work
Nilesh R. Mohite

About the Author

Chandan Pandey is an Oracle Certified Enterprise architect with more than 10 years of experience in designing, coding, and delivering enterprise applications using various tools and technologies. He has always been amused by the power of software that reduces the boredom of repetitive tasks and introduces agility and efficiency. He firmly believes that tools, technology, and methodology are a medium to provide a solution and would like to be positioned as a solutions expert rather than limiting his identity to a framework or tool. This is reflected in the breadth and depth of his work; he is proficient not only in traditional languages and frameworks such as Java/JEE and Spring, but also in Groovy and Grails, Vaadin, and Play Framework, to name a few. His domain experience varies from blogging applications, web frameworks, content management systems, and finance, to networking & telecom. For him, the end result should be extendable, scalable, secure, and easy-to-use systems!

He believes in community ecosystems and tries to share his learning with larger audiences. He writes regularly at www.chandanpandey.com, and this book is a step forward to connect with the community.

When he is not working or writing, he likes to go on road trips with his family to explore new avenues—be it spiritual, historical, or just a leisure tour! India being his home country, he is never short of surprises and variety!

Acknowledgments

I would like to thank the team at Packt Publishing. Richard, thanks a lot for finding my blog on Spring Integration and presenting me with an opportunity to share my knowledge in a more formal way and with a wider audience, and thanks for answering all of my questions with such patience—a few of which often took pages! I would like to thank Sharvari and Ritika, who are the content development editors for this book. Sharvari's support and help with the technical review and incorporation of subsequent feedback was unprecedented. Aman Preet, the technical editor of the book, did a brilliant job with the final edit.

The greatest support is not what we see but the silent love and prayers of all our well-wishers. My parents' blessings have always been with me. They are not technical and they do not understand what I do—but their unflinching confidence in me that *whatever I am doing must be correct* not only pumps up my confidence, but also puts a lot of responsibility on me. I hope I will not disappoint them ever.

Without a supportive family, it's extremely difficult to achieve anything significant—and I consider myself lucky on that front. I am indebted to the charming smiles of my 2-year-old son, Aadish, and my 4-year-old daughter, Aashirya—their innocent smiles always remind me that happiness is beyond material success or anything else. As for my better half, Priyanka, I honestly believe that her work is more creditable than mine. Bringing up two small kids without any help from me, while at the same time supporting me throughout this assignment—a simple "thanks" will be too small a word for her, so I will leave it up to her to understand my gratitude!

About the Reviewers

Marten Deinum is a Java/software consultant working for Conspect. He has developed and architected software, primarily in Java, for small and large companies. He is an enthusiastic open source user and a longtime fan, user, and advocate of the Spring Framework. He has held a number of positions, including that of a software engineer, development lead, coach, and a Java and Spring trainer. He has also authored the book *Pro Spring MVC: with Web Flow*, published by *APress*.

When not working or answering questions on StackOverflow, he can be found in water, training for triathlons or under the water, diving or guiding other people around.

Xinyu Liu graduated from George Washington University, Washington, D.C. He has worked for healthcare companies, a state government agency, and a leading e-commerce company with over 12 years' intensive application design and development experience. During his years of service, new application design and implementation methodologies and strategies were established due to his efforts. His skills cover broad domains such as web development, enterprise application integration, and big data analytics. He writes for Java.net, Javaworld. com, IBM developerWorks, and developer.com on a variety of topics, including web technologies, web security, persistence technologies, rule engine, and big data. In addition, he worked on the review of the books *Spring Web Flow 2 Web Development*, *Grails 1.1 Web Application Development*, and *Application Development for IBM WebSphere Process Server 7 and Enterprise Service Bus 7*, all published by Packt Publishing.

Special thanks to my son, Gavin Liu, and my wife, Xiaowen Zhou.

Luca Masini is a senior software engineer and architect, born as a game developer for Commodore 64 (Football Manager) and Commodore Amiga (Ken il guerriero). He soon converted to object-oriented programming and was attracted by the Java language since its early days in 1995.

He worked on this passion for Java as a consultant for major Italian banks, developing and integrating the main software projects for which he has often taken the technical leadership. He made them adopt Java Enterprise in environments where COBOL was the flagship platform, converting them from mainframe-centric to distributed.

He then shifted his focus toward open source, starting with Linux and then enterprise frameworks with which he was able to introduce concepts such as IoC, ORM, and MVC with low impact. He was an early adopter of Spring, Hibernate, Struts, and a whole host of other technologies that gave his customers a technological advantage and therefore development cost cuts in the long run.

After introducing these new technologies, he decided that it was time for the simplification and standardization of development with Java EE. So, he's now working in the ICT department of a large Italian company where he introduced build tools (Maven and Continuous Integration), archetypes of project, and Agile development with plain standards.

Now, his attention is focused on "mobilizing" the enterprise and he is working on a whole set of standard and development processes to introduce mobile concepts and applications for sales force and management.

He has worked on the following books by Packt Publishing:

- *Securing WebLogic Server 12c*
- *Google Web Toolkit*
- *Spring Web Flow 2*
- *Spring Persistence with Hibernate*
- *Spring Batch Essentials*

www.PacktPub.com

Support files, eBooks, discount offers, and more

For support files and downloads related to your book, please visit www.PacktPub.com.

Did you know that Packt offers eBook versions of every book published, with PDF and ePub files available? You can upgrade to the eBook version at www.PacktPub.com and as a print book customer, you are entitled to a discount on the eBook copy. Get in touch with us at service@packtpub.com for more details.

At www.PacktPub.com, you can also read a collection of free technical articles, sign up for a range of free newsletters and receive exclusive discounts and offers on Packt books and eBooks.

https://www2.packtpub.com/books/subscription/packtlib

Do you need instant solutions to your IT questions? PacktLib is Packt's online digital book library. Here, you can search, access, and read Packt's entire library of books.

Why subscribe?

- Fully searchable across every book published by Packt
- Copy and paste, print, and bookmark content
- On demand and accessible via a web browser

Free access for Packt account holders

If you have an account with Packt at www.PacktPub.com, you can use this to access PacktLib today and view 9 entirely free books. Simply use your login credentials for immediate access.

"I would like to dedicate this work to my late grandmother. She was a living example of unconditional love, integrity, and truthfulness. May god give me enough strength and wisdom to build a character and live a life like hers!"

Table of Contents

Preface

Software has been an integral part of enterprises and a key contributor to their growth. Be it analytics, user experience, social marketing, decision support systems, or any other functional domain, software has been used to aid smooth and efficient functioning. Enterprises start small and grow over a period of time, and so does their software dependency. Enterprise applications are developed over a period of time. The following aspects pose certain challenges while dealing with enterprise software:

- They are distributed across a set of domains, for example, payroll, inventory, reporting, and social integration.

- Each of these modules might have been developed independent of each other and may be on different platforms, for example, employee self-portal in J2EE stack, legacy records management on mainframes, CRM system using Salesforce, with some real-time application in their proprietary implementation.

- These modules need to interact with each other and with external systems as well. They may have to consume data from external sources through SOAP services or shared files, or they themselves have to share data though one of many data-sharing techniques.

- As software grows old, we need to introduce new platforms and replace existing modules to alleviate the growing maintenance cost. A rip and replace strategy would not work; rather, this should be done in a homogenous way without disturbing the sanity of existing modules during the transitions.

Integration of these modules either inside organizations or with external partners is inherently complex, requiring integration of heterogeneous endpoints. This is the kind of scenario that Enterprise Application Integration tries to address. **Enterprise Integration Patterns (EIP)** is a collection of standard enterprise challenges and how can they be handled. Spring Integration is one of the implementations of the EIP that provides many off-the-shelf components recommended by EIP.

How enterprise integration challenges can be solved

Many approaches have been tried to make the integration simple without compromising on vital aspects of enterprise, such as security, transaction, availability, reliability, and so on. A few of the prominent methodologies used over time are **Java Connector Architecture (JCA)**, RMI, RPC, and CORBA for platform-agnostic integration, message brokers with system adapter, and many more. Under the hood, they try to solve integration issues through one of the following techniques:

- **Shared File**: This is the simplest approach. Systems can write data in a predefined format to a file, which can be read by other endpoints. An adapter might be needed to convert a format between two different endpoints. Let's consider an example, a daily report used to be generated in a CSV file. Over time, the organization established a web presence and reports need to be pushed online now. How can this be achieved? The simplest way is to dump it in files that will be read by an adapter and fed into the CMS system. A filesystem is simple but not the best solution; it is not transactional. What if a particular file is corrupt, or what if at poll interval files are not available due to network failure? This necessitates the introduction of a complex system that has a retry mechanism, filter capabilities, and many more nonfunctional aspects such as secure access, archival, and so on.

- **Shared database**: This addresses a few of the challenges that are addressed by the filesystem, such as transactional behavior, role-based access, performance tuning, distributed support, and so on. The common mechanism is a set of join tables — one application writes data in a schema that is understood by others. On the flip side, this introduces tight coupling; if there is a change in schema, both the systems need to be updated accordingly. Evolving applications will become a challenge, as they will have to factor in the external system limitations. The integration effort might itself start with lot of hiccups, for example, compatibility issues between the SQL provided by database vendors of the application, data format, and types in their table. For example, if one system stores only the date while the other stores the date with time stamp, depending on need, at least one will have to change format.

- **Remote procedure calls**: This mechanism introduces a paradigm where each system can offer services by publishing the contract. These paradigms can be a method, parameters, result, and error. For example, an EJB service or a SOAP service can be exposed for providing raw data for a reporting module that renders it in multiple formats. The most limiting aspect is synchronous behavior, where systems have to wait for the result. There are other challenges such as serialization of data, network latency, performance issues of a module, which can bring down the whole application, and so on. From a security aspect, exposing the method name and parameter invites hackers to exercise their creativity.

- **Messaging**: This introduces the asynchronous model in which two heterogeneous modules can interact through data over a predefined connection. The greatest advantage is decoupling—none of the systems are dependent on the availability of the other and they can participate or withdraw from integration without impacting other components. JMS is an example of message-based integration. Spring Integration is based on this paradigm where multiple endpoints connect on to a channel, produce or consume messages, and perform further processing based on information in a message. We will deal with channel, endpoints, message payload, and other concepts in the upcoming chapters.

Even if we use one of the preceding techniques, enterprise systems are way outward from each other and all of them might not be working all the time. This necessitated the use of middleware that can orchestrate reliable communication between these disparate endpoints, typically called an **Enterprise Service Bus (ESB)**. In layman's terms, ESB can be defined as the middle man who enables communication to and fro between heterogeneous interfaces.

Who are the players?

As we have been discussing, the problem of enterprise integration is complex and many vendors have tried to address it in their own propitiatory ESB framework—earlier it used to be dominated by commercial vendors such as Tibco, Vitria, IBM MQSeries, Oracle SOA Suite, Microsoft BizTalk, and so on. Over time, the need for open source frameworks became evident as smaller organizations grew. Their integration needs were limited and were incapable of investing upfront with any of these biggies.

Some of the prominent open source integration frameworks, apart from Spring Integration, are Camel, Service Mix, Mule ESB, Open ESB, and so on. A comprehensive comparison of these frameworks is beyond the scope of this book but a small summary of two other major open source frameworks, has been provided here for the sake of emphasizing Spring Integration simplicity:

- **Mule ESB**: It is a standard server, solutions are developed and deployed inside them. Mule is one of the most prominent and stable solutions on the market. The point to be observed here is that, it's a container that holds the application.

- **Service Mix (SM)**: Apache Service Mix is built over JAVA legacy JBI (Java Business Integration). Service Mix tries to solve almost all aspects of enterprise integration by unifying the features and functionality of ActiveMQ, Camel, CXF, ODE, and Karaf. It provides a complete, enterprise-ready ESB, exclusively powered by OSGi. Since it tries to address a lot of modules, it is pretty bulky compared to Spring Integration.

Why Spring Integration?

Spring Integration is an open source effort to address integration challenges; it is based on the Spring Framework, which is the most widely used Java-based framework in organizations. It introduces the simple POJO-based programming model to support standard integration patterns.

It's lightweight; all it needs is couple of jars for which Maven targets are readily available. A quick comparison shows that the Service Mix download is around 55 MB while Spring Integration is just 14 MB in size.

- Spring Integration is just a set of standard Java libraries; the solution gets deployed in the application instead of that application getting deployed in some containers, as in the case of SM and Mule.

For enterprises that are already using Java and Spring, it eases the integration effort as it follows the same idioms and patterns of the Spring Framework.

What this book covers

Chapter 1, Getting Started, explains how to set up the Eclipse IDE, a "Hello World" program, and a brief introduction of how Spring ROO can ease the configuration aspects even further. This will help overcome configuration nightmares and warm up developers to a hands-on experience.

Chapter 2, *Message Ingestion*, introduces channels through which messages can be read and processed. It describes the point-to-point and pub-sub models, which one is best suited for a given scenario, how errors can be handled in a decoupled manner on a channel, and finally how in-memory channels can be backed up with persistence for failover and recovery solutions.

Chapter 3, *Message Processing*, explains how to define components that can apply business logic on messages, introduces decoupled logging that can used for auditing, and discusses adding transactional behavior.

Chapter 4, *Message Transformers*, deals with processing message formats, its conversion to a homogenous format, and how annotations can help keep the configurations clean. Messages can be introduced in heterogeneous formats such as XML, JSON, and so on that need to be converted to a format understood by the system.

Chapter 5, *Message Flow*, will introduce flow aspects to messages such as filtering messages that do not comply to validation rules, routing them to an error branch, splitting messages, and redirecting them to components appropriate for their processing—waiting for incomplete payloads, aggregating partial messages, and finally the chaining of business processing handlers.

Chapter 6, *Integration with External Systems*, will give a hands-on overview of integration points. Integration with external systems is the most interesting and powerful aspect of Spring Integration—interaction with external systems is a matter of a few lines of configuration. Spring Integration has introduced adapters, gateways, and other components that make it a breeze to interact with filesystems, SQL, NoSQL persistence store, HTTP services, and other widely used external entities such as different servers, social media, and so on.

Chapter 7, *Integration with Spring Batch*, will introduce how to use Spring Integration and batch module for scheduling, triggering, and monitoring batch jobs.

Chapter 8, *Testing Support*, will explain how to leverage the readily available mocks for different components, what to test, and how much to test.

Chapter 9, *Monitoring, Management, and Scaling Up*, will cover using Spring Integration configuration to leverage JMX to get performance statistics of different configured components in the system. We will also peek into ways to scale up Spring Integration components.

Chapter 10, *An End-to-End Example*, has an end-to-end hands-on example that will help you to recollect concepts introduced in different chapters and reassert their understanding. Code will be pushed to a social repository as GitHub, but this chapter will give users enough instructions to use it and run it.

What you need for this book

You need a Java-based IDE, and Spring STS is recommended. JDK 1.6 and above is required.

Who this book is for

This book is for developers who are already familiar with basic Java and Spring concepts. Concepts of Enterprise Integration Patterns would be helpful but not mandatory. The book has been presented in a hands-on manner; an end-to-end working example has been picked, implemented, and explained throughout the chapters. This book would serve as a strong companion for new developers trying out their hand on integration aspects, and as a hands-on guide on how to use Spring Integration components for developers already familiar with these challenges and looking for quick samples.

Conventions

In this book, you will find a number of styles of text that distinguish between different kinds of information. Here are some examples of these styles, and an explanation of their meaning.

Code words in text, database table names, folder names, filenames, file extensions, pathnames, dummy URLs, user input, and Twitter handles are shown as follows: "Create a Spring Integration project by navigating to **File | Spring Project**, as shown in the following screenshot:".

A block of code is set as follows:

```
<int:channel id="resultPersistenceChannel">
  <int:queue message-store="messageStore"/>
</int:channel>

<int-jdbc:message-store id="messageStore" data-
  source="someDataSource"/>
```

When we wish to draw your attention to a particular part of a code block, the relevant lines or items are set in bold:

```
public interface ChannelInterceptor {
  Message<?> preSend(Message<?> message, MessageChannel channel);
  void postSend(Message<?> message, MessageChannel channel,
boolean sent);
  boolean preReceive(MessageChannel channel);
  Message<?> postReceive(Message<?> message, MessageChannel
    channel);
```

New terms and **important words** are shown in bold. Words that you see on the screen, in menus or dialog boxes for example, appear in the text like this: "clicking the **Next** button moves you to the next screen".

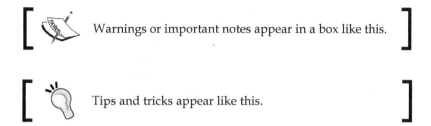

Warnings or important notes appear in a box like this.

Tips and tricks appear like this.

Reader feedback

Feedback from our readers is always welcome. Let us know what you think about this book—what you liked or may have disliked. Reader feedback is important for us to develop titles that you really get the most out of.

To send us general feedback, simply send an e-mail to feedback@packtpub.com, and mention the book title via the subject of your message.

If there is a topic that you have expertise in and you are interested in either writing or contributing to a book, see our author guide on www.packtpub.com/authors.

Customer support

Now that you are the proud owner of a Packt book, we have a number of things to help you to get the most from your purchase.

Downloading the example code

You can download the example code files for all Packt books you have purchased from your account at http://www.packtpub.com. If you purchased this book elsewhere, you can visit http://www.packtpub.com/support and register to have the files e-mailed directly to you. The code can also be pulled from https://github.com/cpandey05/siessentials.

Errata

Although we have taken every care to ensure the accuracy of our content, mistakes do happen. If you find a mistake in one of our books—maybe a mistake in the text or the code—we would be grateful if you would report this to us. By doing so, you can save other readers from frustration and help us improve subsequent versions of this book. If you find any errata, please report them by visiting http://www.packtpub.com/submit-errata, selecting your book, clicking on the **errata submission form** link, and entering the details of your errata. Once your errata are verified, your submission will be accepted and the errata will be uploaded on our website, or added to any list of existing errata, under the Errata section of that title. Any existing errata can be viewed by selecting your title from http://www.packtpub.com/support.

Piracy

Piracy of copyright material on the Internet is an ongoing problem across all media. At Packt, we take the protection of our copyright and licenses very seriously. If you come across any illegal copies of our works, in any form, on the Internet, please provide us with the location address or website name immediately so that we can pursue a remedy.

Please contact us at copyright@packtpub.com with a link to the suspected pirated material.

We appreciate your help in protecting our authors, and our ability to bring you valuable content.

Questions

You can contact us at questions@packtpub.com if you are having a problem with any aspect of the book, and we will do our best to address it.

1
Getting Started

In this chapter, we will set up our development environment and discuss how we can leverage **SpringSource Tool Suite** (**STS**) to its maximum. Although any popular Java development IDE such as *Eclipse*, *intelliJ*, *NetBeans*, and others can be used for developing Spring Integration solutions, pivotal, the company spearheading Spring Integration, recommends that you use **STS** which is an Eclipse-based IDE.

Setting up STS

STS comes with many off-the-shelf plugins, visual editors, and other features, which ease the development of Spring-powered enterprise applications. The look and feel of the IDE is very similar to Eclipse. Install STS by following these steps:

1. JDK 1.6 and above is a prerequisite, download and install it from `http://www.oracle.com/technetwork/java/javase/downloads/java-archive-downloads-javase6-419409.html`.

2. Set `JAVA_HOME` properties as explained in the documentation at `https://docs.oracle.com/cd/E19182-01/820-7851/inst_cli_jdk_javahome_t/index.html`.

3. Download STS from `http://spring.io/tools/sts`.

4. The downloaded file is in ZIP format. Extract it to the preferred folder and it's all set.

5. Go to `<installation-directory>\sts-bundle\sts-3.6.1.RELEASE`. The `STS.exe` file is the executable for launching the IDE.

6. This step is optional but can help in efficient functioning of the OS editor — change the memory allocation parameter. Locate `STS.ini` (in the same folder as `STS.exe`) and change the value of `Xmx`. For 2 GB, I've put it as `Xmx2048m`.

Creating your first project

The following steps will help you in creating your first project:

1. Create a Spring Integration project by navigating to **File** | **Spring Project**, as shown in the following screenshot:

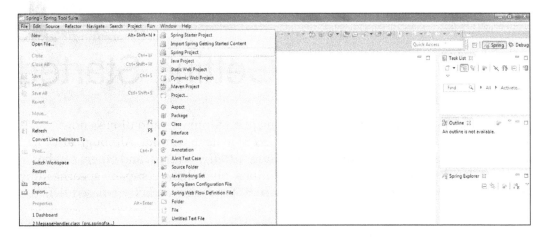

2. Under the templates section, select **Spring Integration Project - Simple**. Provide a project name, for example, `sisimple`, as shown in the following screenshot:

3. Fill in the information required to create a Maven-based project, as shown in this screenshot:

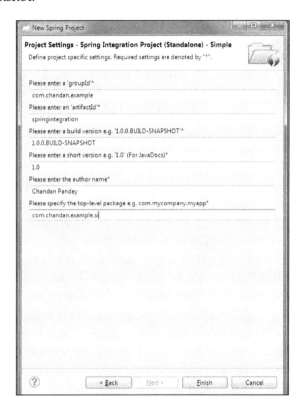

4. Click on **Finish**; this will create a project with the name that was provided by us (`sisimple`), as shown in this screenshot:

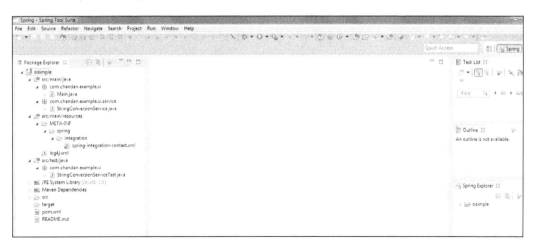

This project is as simple as it can be. Let's take a quick look at the generated Java classes in the following points:

- `Main.java`: This file is located at the path: `/sisimple/src/main/java/com/chandan/example/si/`. It has the main method and will be used to run this sample. Right-click on this file from the package explorer and click on **Run As | Java Application** — this will start the program. This class has the code to bootstrap Spring Integration configuration files and load components defined in it. Additionally, it converts user input to upper case.

- `StringConversionService.java`: This file is located at the path: `/sisimple/src/main/java/com/chandan/example/si/service/`. This is the service interface that is used to convert user input to upper case.

- `spring-integration-context.xml`: This file is located at the path: `/sisimple/src/main/resources/META-INF/spring/integration/`. It is the Spring Integration configuration file. It contains the XML-based declaration of Spring Integration components.

- `log4j.xml`: This file is located at the path: `/sisimple/src/main/resources/`. It is the `Log4j` configuration file. It can be edited to control the log level, appenders, and other logging-related aspects.

- `StringConversionServiceTest.java`: This file is located at the path: `/sisimple/src/test/java/com/chandan/example/si/`. This is the test file for `StringConversionService`. This will be used to run tests against the service classes.

- `pom.xml`: This is the file used for rmaven dependency management, located in `/sisimple/`. It has entries for all the dependencies used by the project.

It will be a bit heavy and premature to explain each of the components in these classes and configuration files without having built up some theoretical concepts — we will discuss each of the elements in detail, as we move ahead in the chapters.

STS visual editor

STS provides visual ways to add different namespaces. Locate `spring-integration-context.xml` under `/sisimple/src/main/resources/META-INF/spring/integration/` and open it. This is the default Spring configuration file. Click on the **Namespaces** tab to manage different namespaces of Spring Integration. The following screenshot shows imported namespaces for this sample project:

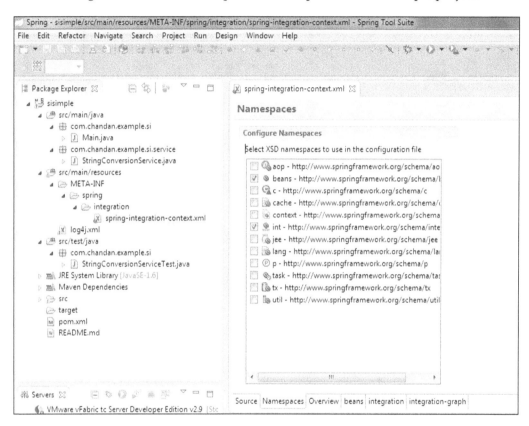

In the same editor, clicking on the **Integration-graph** tab will open a visual editor, which can be used to add/modify or delete endpoints, channels, and other components of Spring Integration. The following screenshot contains the integration graph for our sample project:

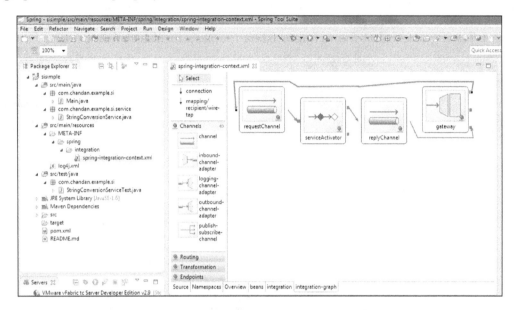

Let's have a quick look at the generated Maven POM — overall, there are three dependencies; only one for Spring Integration, and the other ones for *Junit* and *log4j*, as shown in the following screenshot:

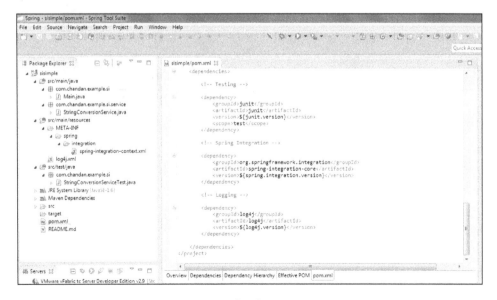

Spring Integration Scala DSL

This is still in the very early stages and is an incubation project. Scala DSL should not be confused with other EIP implementations being offered in Scala — rather, it is built on top of Spring Integration and provides DSL-based configuration and flow management.

 Check out the official Spring Integration Scala DSL blog at `http://spring.io/blog/2012/03/05/ introducing-spring-integration-scala- dsl/` and the GitHub page at `https://github. com/spring-projects/spring-integration- dsl-groovy`.

Summary

In this chapter, you learned how to set up your IDE and created a basic project. We also tried our hands at the visual editor of STS and covered a quick introduction of the upcoming Scala DSL for Spring Integration. We will leverage this knowledge to build a compelling Spring Integration application using STS throughout the rest of the chapters.

In the next chapter, we will cover how to ingest messages in the application and then how to process them.

2
Message Ingestion

As mentioned in the *Preface*, Spring Integration is an implementation of *Enterprise Integration Patterns: Designing, Building, and Deploying Messaging Solutions (Addison Wesley Signature Series)*, *Gregor Hohpe* and *Bobby Woolf*, *Addison-Wesley Professional*. **EIP** (short for **Enterprise Integration Patterns**) defines patterns for many integration challenges, and one of them is the exchange of messages between heterogeneous systems. In this chapter, we will explore patterns and concepts around message exchange.

Heterogeneous endpoints use messaging to communicate. There are primarily three aspects of messaging: messages being exchanged, the endpoints that participate in the communication, and the medium through which messages are delivered. In an EIP paradigm, we define them as messages, message endpoints, and message channels. Let's discuss each one at a time and then we will discuss the pattern.

What is a message? In simplest terms, messages can be understood as a piece of information that can be used as an enabler for intercommunication and collaboration between heterogeneous components. It is composed of primarily two parts: header and payload. Headers contain metadata and commonly require values such as ID, timestamp, and so on, but a header's use can be extended for passing other values as well, for example, a channel name for a router, file components for a filename, and so on. Payload can be of any type: standard Java object, XML, or any custom or user-defined value. It can be a simple information-sharing payload too (for example, a registration module can notify an audit module when a new user is registered), or it can be a command (for example, an administration module can instruct the mail service to notify all the users who've registered for the course), or it can be an event (for example, a mail service that, after sending all the mails, dispatches an event back to the admin module specifying that all the mails have been sent and it's good to go with the next step).

We noticed a pattern here; there is a communication between two components via these messages — in formal terms, we call these components message endpoints. Similarly, we can observe that message endpoints are of two types: producer endpoint and consumer endpoint. As their names suggest, a producer, such as `registration module`, generates a message in the given example, while a consumer consumes it — for example the `audit module` in the given example. An endpoint can be a producer as well as a consumer, for example, a mail service. Endpoints are typically smart components that can validate messages before passing them on to the next subsystem or can route, filter, aggregate, transform, or do a lot more so that the message can be in a format expected by the next in the chain.

Working with message channels

We defined messages and we discussed how message endpoints act on the messages, so where does a message channel fit in? A message channel is an implementation of the EAI design pattern that decouples the endpoint. Endpoints do not need to be aware of each other's type; they register with channels and it's the responsibility of the channel to deliver the messages safely between endpoints. Each channel has a logical identity — it may be a unique name or ID through which it can be referred and registered to. Depending on how channels handle the messages, they can be classified in two broad categories:

* Point-to-point channel
* Publish-subscribe channel

Channel types

Before starting with their implementation, let's first look at the following types of channels:

* **Point-to-point channel**: A one-to-one relationship is maintained between producer and consumer. These channels deliver message to one and only one recipient. Even if more than one recipient is registered, messages will only be delivered to one of them. This channel type can be used in a parallel processing scenario, allowing multiple consumers to listen to the availability of messages in parallel, but the delivery of messages will be done to a single consumer only!
* **Publish-subscribe channel**: These channels deliver messages to all of the subscribers who have registered on the channel, thus implementing a one-to-many relationship between producer and consumer. An analogy can be drawn as each subscriber has its own private channel, on which a copy of the message is delivered. As soon as it's consumed, it is discarded.

Let's get out of idioms and have a sneak peek at how Spring Integration provides support for all of these components—after all, this is a book on Spring Integration, isn't it!

Spring implementation of channels

Spring Integration defines a top-level interface for the message channel that should be implemented by any of the concrete channel implementations, as shown here:

```
public interface MessageChannel {
  boolean send(Message<?> message);
  boolean send(Message<?> message, long timeout);
}
```

The `MessageChannel` interface defines two versions of the `send` method—one which accepts only `Message` as an argument while the other one accepts an additional parameter (`timeout`). The `send` method returns true if the message is sent out successfully; otherwise, if it times out or the sending fails for some reason, it returns false.

Further, Spring Integration provides a sub type of the `MessageChannel` interface to support two types of channels: `PollableChannel` and `SubscribableChannel`. This is explained in more detail in the following points:

- **Pollable channel**: This channel provides the interface that has two versions of receive, one which does not take any argument and the other which provides an option to specify the `timeout` parameter. The following code snippet is the interface declaration:

  ```
  public interface PollableChannel extends MessageChannel {
    Message<?> receive();
    Message<?> receive(long timeout);
  }
  ```

- **Subscribeable channel**: This interface exposes methods to subscribe and unsubscribe from the channel. The following code snippet is the interface declaration for a subscribe-able channel:

  ```
  public interface SubscribableChannel extends MessageChannel {
    boolean subscribe(MessageHandler handler);
    boolean unsubscribe(MessageHandler handler);
  }
  ```

An instance of the `MessageHandler` interface is passed as an argument to the `subscribe` and `unsubscribe` methods. The `MessageHandler` interface exposes only one method, `handleMessage`, to handle the message:

```
public interface MessageHandler {
    void handleMessage(Message<?> message) throws MessageException;
}
```

Whenever a message arrives on a channel, an implementation of the message handler is looked upon by the framework, and the message is passed to the implementer's `handleMessage` method.

Although Spring Integration defines message channel interfaces and allows users to provide their implementation, it's hardly ever needed. Spring Integration has provided many implementations of channels that can be used *off the shelf*.

Selecting a channel

Let's discuss what default implementations have been provided by Spring Integration and how they can be leveraged.

Publish-subscribe channel

This is the only implementation of the publish-subscribe model of channel. The primary purpose of this channel is to send messages to registered endpoints; this cannot be polled. It can be declared as follows:

```
<int:publish-subscribe-channel id="pubSubChannel"/>
```

Let's discuss each of the elements in this line; this will be used throughout the examples of this chapter:

- `int`: This is a namespace that declares all Spring Integration components. As discussed in *Chapter 1, Getting Started*, the STS visual editor can be used to add different namespaces from Spring Integration.
- `publish-subscribe-channel`: This is the type exposed by Spring.
- `Id`: This is the unique name through which the channel can be referred.

To refer to these elements from the code, we can use:

```
public class PubSubExample {
    private ApplicationContext ctx = null;
    private MessageChannel pubSubChannel = null;
    public PubSubChannelTest() {
```

```
        ctx = new ClassPathXmlApplicationContext
          ("spring-integration-context.xml");
        pubSubChannel = ctx.getBean
          ("pubSubChannel", MessageChannel.class);
    }
}
```

Queue channel

Remember queue concepts from good old data structures? QueueChannel employs the same concept—it enforces **First in First out (FIFO)** ordering and a message can be consumed by one and only one endpoint. It's a strictly one-to-one relationship, even if the channel has multiple consumers; one message will be delivered to only one of them. In Spring Integration, it can be defined as follows:

```
<int:channel id="queueChannel">
  <queue capacity="50"/>
</int:channel>
```

As soon as a message is available on the channel, it will try to send the message to the subscribed consumer. The element capacity indicates the maximum number of undelivered messages to be held in the queue. If the queue is full, which is determined by the capacity parameter, the sender will be blocked until messages are consumed and further room is available in the queue. Alternatively, if a timeout parameter has been specified for the sender, the sender will wait for the specified timeout interval—if space is created in the queue within the timeout interval, the sender will put the message there, else it will discard that message and start with another one.

 Although capacity parameter is optional, it should never be left out; otherwise, the queue will become unbounded and may result in OutOfMemoryErrors.

Priority channel

Queue enforces FIFO, but what if a message needs urgent attention and needs to be processed out of the queue? For example, a server health monitoring service might send health audits to an *audit service*, but if it sends a server down event, it needs urgent processing. This is where PriorityChannel is handy; it can pick messages based on their priority rather than arrival order. Messages can be prioritized as follows:

- By adding a priority header within each message
- By providing a comparator of type Comparator<Message<?>> to the priority channel's constructor

Default is the `priority` header in the message.

Let's take the following example of a priority channel and inject a comparator there, which will be used to decide the priority of the message:

```
<int:channel id="priorityChannel">
  <int:priority-queue capacity="50"/>
</int:channel>
```

A comparator can be injected as follows:

```
<int:channel id="priorityChannel" datatype="com.example.result">
  <int:priority-queue comparator="resultComparator"
    capacity="50"/>
</int:channel>
```

Rendezvous channel

Often, it is desirable to have an acknowledgement that the message has indeed reached the endpoint. The `rendezvousChannel` interface, which is a subclass of the queue channel, serves this purpose. Producer and consumer work in a blocking mode. As soon as the producer sends a message on the channel, it is blocked until that message has been consumed. Similarly, a consumer is blocked until a message arrives in the queue. It can be configured as follows:

```
<int:channel id="rendezvousChannel"/>
  <int:rendezvous-queue/>
</int:channel>
```

The `RendezvousChannel` interface implements a zero capacity queue, which means that at any given point, there can exist only one message on the queue. No wonder there is no capacity element.

Direct channel

Direct channel is the default channel type used by Spring Integration.

 When using the `<channel/>` element without any subelements, it will create a `DirectChannel` instance (a `SubscribableChannel`) handler.

Multiple endpoints can subscribe message handlers with the direct channel; whenever a producer puts a message on the channel, it is delivered to one and only one of the message handlers of subscribed endpoints. The introduction of multiple subscribers with a restriction to deliver a message to one and only one of the handlers introduces new challenges—how and which handler will be selected and what will happen if the handler is not able to process the message? This is where a load balancer and failover come into the picture. A load balancer can be defined on this channel with a round-robin delivery strategy:

```
<int:channel id="newQuestions">
  <dispatcher failover="false" load-balancer="round-robin"/>
</int:channel>
```

This will deliver messages to subscribers on a round-robin basis. This is the only strategy defined out-of-the-box by Spring, but a custom strategy can be defined using `interface`:

```
public interface LoadBalancingStrategy {
  public Iterator<MessageHandler> getHandlerIterator(
  Message<?> message, List<MessageHandler> handlers);
}
```

Here is an example of introducing a custom load balancer:

```
<int:channel id="lbChannel">
  <int:dispatcher load-balancer-ref="customLb"/>
</int:channel>

<bean id="customLb" class="com.chandan.CustomLoadBalancingImpl"/>
```

Downloading the example code

You can download the example code files for all Packt books you have purchased from your account at http://www.packtpub.com. If you purchased this book elsewhere, you can visit http://www. packtpub.com/support and register to have the files e-mailed directly to you. The code can also be pulled from https://github. com/cpandey05/siessentials.

Failover, on other hand, is a Boolean value. If this is set to true, then if the first handler fails to process the message, then all subsequent handlers will be tried. Even if one of the handlers successfully processes the message, Spring Integration will not report an error. Only if all of the handlers fail, will it throw an exception.

Failover capability can be very handy while implementing a transaction propagation or for a fallback mechanism. For example, if a DB server fails, try another backend server in the next handler.

Executor channel

The `ExecutorChannel` interface is a point-to-point message channel. This is very similar to the direct channel, except that custom executors can be used to dispatch the messages. Let's have a look at the configuration:

```
<int:channel id="results">
<int:dispatcher task-executor="resultExecutor"/></int:channel>
// define the executor
<bean id=" resultExecutor " class="com.example.ResultExecutor"/>
```

The `com.example.ResultExecutor` interface is an implementation of `java.uti.concurrent.Executor`.

A transaction link cannot be established between producer and consumer because a producer thread hands off the message to an executor instance and backs off—the consumption of the message is processed in the executor thread.

As in direct channels, a load-balancing strategy and failover can be set. The default values are a round-robin strategy with failover enabled:

```
<int:channel id="results">
<int:dispatcher load-balancer="none" failover="false"
  taskexecutor="resultsExecutor"/>
</int:channel>
```

Scoped channel

When a channel is declared, it is in a global space and visible to all of the threads. But what if we want to restrict the visibility of the channel to a certain scope, such as a particular thread, web session request scope, and so on? The `scope` attribute does just this: it defines the scope in which the channel is visible. For example, a channel defined in the following code snippet is visible in the `thread` scope:

```
<int:channel id="threadScopeChannel" scope="thread">
  <int:queue />
</int:channel>
```

A custom scope can also be defined, as follows:

```
<bean class="org.springframework.beans.factory.config.
  CustomScopeConfigurer">
  <property name="scopes">
    <map>
      <entry key="thread"
        value="org.springframework.context.support.
        SimpleThreadScope" />
```

```
      </map>
    </property>
  </bean>
```

This is an example of a thread scoped channel. If we observe the entries, a key-value pair has been defined for the scope. For the thread, the key-value pair is `org.springframework.context.support.SimpleThreadScope`. It can be any Spring-defined or a user-defined scope.

Some of the other Spring implemented scopes are as follows:

- `org.springframework.web.context.request.SessionScope`
- `org.springframework.web.context.support.ServletContextScope`
- `org.springframework.web.context.request.RequestScope`
- `org.springframework.web.portlet.context.PortletContextScope`

Datatype channel

A channel can be restricted to accept messages having only a certain type of payload, for example, numbers, string, or any other custom type. The code is as follows:

```
<int:channel id="examMarksChannel" datatype="java.lang.Number"/>
```

Multiple types can also be provided, as follows:

```
<int:channel id="stringOrNumberChannel"
  datatype="java.lang.String,java.lang.Number"/>
```

What will happen if a message arrives in a format other than the one given in the preceding code? By default, an exception will be thrown. However, if the use case warrants, we can define converters, which will try to convert incoming messages into an acceptable format. A typical use case is the conversion of a string to an integer. For this to happen, a bean named `integrationConversionService` that is an instance of Spring's Conversion Service must be defined as follows:

```
public static class StringToIntegerConverter implements
Converter<String, Integer> {
  public Integer convert(String source) {
    return Integer.parseInt(source);
  }
}
```

```
<int:converter ref="strToInt"/>

<bean id="strToInt" class="com.chandan.StringToIntegerConverter"/>
```

When the `converter` element is parsed, it will create the `integrationConversionService` bean on-demand, if one is not already defined. With that converter in place, if a string message arrives on a channel defined as an integer, an attempt would be made to convert it to an integer.

Error handling on channels

Spring Integration supports synchronous as well as asynchronous message processing. In the case of synchronous processing, it is comparatively easy to handle error scenarios based on return values or by catching thrown exceptions; for asynchronous processing, things are more complicated. There are components provided by Spring, such as filters and routers, that can be used to validate message sanity and take action based on that. If it's invalid, the message can be routed to an invalid channel or a retry channel as the case may be. Apart from this, Spring provides a global error channel and capability to define custom error channels. The following points cover an appropriate error channel:

- An error channel needs to be defined. This can be done as follows:
  ```
  <int:channel id="invalidMarksErrorChannel">
    <int:queue capacity="500"/>
  </int:channel>
  ```

- A header named `errorChannel` needs to be added to the message. This is the name of the channel where `ErrorMessage` should be routed when processing fails.

- If message processing fails, `ErrorMessage` will be sent to the channel specified by the header `errorChannel`.

- If the message does not contain a `errorChanel` header, `ErrorMessage` will be routed to a global error channel defined by Spring Integration, which is `errorChannel`. This channel is a publish-subscribe channel:
  ```
  <int:gateway default-request-channel="questionChannel"
    service-interface="com.chandan.processQuestion"
    error-channel="errorChannel"/>
  ```

Persisting and recovering channels

We talked about all kind of channels, but if you have noticed, these are all in memory. What if the system crashes? No one wants to lose data. This is where persistent `QueueChannel` comes into the picture—messages will be backed up in the database defined by the data source. If the system crashes, then on recovery, it will pull all the messages in the database and queue them for processing. This is achieved in Spring using `MessageGroupStore`. Let's have a quick look at the configuration:

```
<int:channel id="resultPersistenceChannel">
  <int:queue message-store="messageStore"/>
</int:channel>

<int-jdbc:message-store id="messageStore" data-
  source="someDataSource"/>
```

Here, the message store is mapped to the database defined by `someDataSource`. When a message arrives, it will now be added to `MessageStore` first. On successful processing, it will be removed from there.

The moment we talk of databases, transaction comes into the picture. So what if the poller has a transaction configured? In that case, if message processing fails, the transaction will be rolled backed and the message will not be deleted from the queue.

> If transactional behavior is supported, messages will not be removed from the queue until they have been successfully processed. If some messages fail repeatedly, this may build up stale messages in the queue over time. A clean-up strategy for such messages must be thought through.

Channel interceptors

Interceptor patterns can be used to apply business rules and validations on messages that are either sent from the channel or received on it. The following four interceptors are available:

```
public interface ChannelInterceptor {
  Message<?> preSend(Message<?> message, MessageChannel channel);
  void postSend(Message<?> message, MessageChannel channel,
    boolean sent);
  boolean preReceive(MessageChannel channel);
  Message<?> postReceive(Message<?> message, MessageChannel
    channel);
}
```

Adding an interceptor is straightforward: define a class that implements the `ChannelInterceptor` interface and then inject a reference of it in the channel definition. Here is a quick code snippet to show this:

```
<int:channel id="resultChannel">
  <int:interceptors>
    <ref bean="resultValidationInterceptor"/>
  </int:interceptors>
</int:channel>
```

Here are the methods exposed by the `ChannelInterceptor` interface:

- `preSend`: This is invoked before a message is sent. A null value should be returned if the message is blocked from sending.

- `postSend`: This is invoked after an attempt to send a message. It indicates whether the message was sent successfully or not. This can be used for audit purposes.

- `preReceive`: This applies only if the channel is pollable and is invoked when a component calls `receive()` on the channel, but before a message is actually read from that channel. It allows implementers to decide whether the channel can return a message to the caller.

- `postReceive`: This is similar to `preReceive` and it applies only to pollable channels. It's invoked after a message is read from a channel but before it's returned to the component that called `receive()`. If it returns a null value, then no message is received. This allows the implementer to control what, if anything, is actually received by the poller.

Summary

This is a comparatively long chapter in which we discussed message channel patterns, different types of channels, and the default implementations of channels provided by Spring. We also covered load balancing, failover, error handling on message channels, persisting messages, and adding interceptors. All these concepts are at the core of building a reliable and scalable solution, and we will see its hands-on implementation in the upcoming chapters where we will discuss Spring Integration components such as service activators, gateway, delayers, and so on that are used to process messages.

3
Message Processing

In *Chapter 1, Getting Started*, we discussed that the need for enterprise integration was evolved to solve the problem of intercommunication between heterogeneous systems: how will they share data, how will they understand other systems' data, how cross-cutting concerns across applications will be handled, and so on. In the previous chapter, we covered one of the aspects, that is, how the systems will exchange data. Channels provide a logical unit over which data can be dropped off for other interested applications. However, it introduces the next set of challenges: what if the format of data is not understandable by other modules, or what if the rate of producing a message versus the rate of consuming it is different? Let's take an example; an RSS feed needs to be fetched from the Internet and put in a database for reporting, as well as on a mailing system to send out mails about the availability of new items. What challenges does it throw?

- The RSS feed is in the XML format, while for databases and mail it needs to be converted to the Java entity and the Java `MailMessage` format, respectively (assuming JPA and java mail is being used). This means the XML payload needs to be translated into the format expected by the next set of endpoints.

- There could be latency while sending out mails; hence, flooding the mail server might result in loss of messages, indicating the need for throttling.

- Before the message can be handed over to the database, some audit information such as timestamp, user logged in, and others, needs to be augmented.

- There might be some XML payloads that are not valid or may be incomplete. We would like to discard those and retry!

- The mail server might not be available at the time the feed arrived — what to do then?

These points provide a glimpse into a few of the aspects that need to be taken care of when two systems try to communicate. It's definitely not a good idea to load the systems with all this heavy logic and in turn introduce tight coupling between them. Then, who takes care of all of these aspects? Let's welcome message endpoints. In this chapter, we will cover the following topics:

- Message endpoints
- Gateways
- Service activators
- Delayers
- Transactions

Message endpoints

In the simplest analogy, **message endpoints** are enablers that facilitate interaction between two systems—be it transformation of messages, throttling, intermediate business processing, or any other tasks that might be needed for the message to be successfully and seamlessly handled by the next system in the chain. To cater to different needs, different types of message endpoints are available, for example, *enrichers*, *delayers*, *service activators*, and others. However, before diving deep into each specific detail, let's discuss the broad level of categorization for the endpoints:

- **Receivers or senders**: Endpoints can either receive messages from the channel or put messages on the channel for further processing.

- **Polling endpoints or event-driven endpoints**: Endpoints can either pull messages from the channel or can subscribe to it. Whenever a message is available, a registered callback method is called.

- **Unidirectional or bidirectional endpoints**: Unidirectional endpoints send off or receive messages, but do not expect or receive any acknowledgement. Spring Integration provides channel adapters for such types of interactions. Bidirectional adapters can send, receive, and acknowledge messages. Spring Integration provides gateways that are synonymous with synchronous two-way communication.

- **Inbound or outbound endpoints**: Outbound endpoints interact with external systems such as social networks, mail servers, enterprise JMS, and others, whereas inbound endpoints listen for events from outside entities such as mail connector, FTP connector, and so on.

Spring Integration has provided implementation of all of these types; let's explore them.

Gateways

Abstraction and loose coupling is always desired. **Messaging gateways** is a mechanism to publish a contract that can be used by systems without exposing the underlying messaging implementation. For example, a gateway for a mailing subsystem can expose methods for sending and receiving mail. Internally, the implementation can be done using the raw Java mail API, or can be adapters from Spring Integration, or may be some custom implementation altogether. As long as the contract does not change, implementation can be easily switched or enhanced without impacting on the rest of the modules. It is an implementation of more generic *gateway* patterns. Gateways can be of two types: *synchronous* and *asynchronous*.

Synchronous gateways

Let's quickly see what a declaration of a gateway looks like in Spring Integration, and then decimate it further to build our understanding:

```
<int:gateway id="feedService"
  service-interface="com.cpandey.siexample.service.FeedService"
  default-request-channel="requestChannel"
  default-reply-channel="replyChannel"/>
```

This basic code defines a gateway in Spring. Let's understand the preceding declaration:

- `int:gateway`: This is the Spring framework namespace for gateway
- `service-interface`: This is an interface that is the contract published by the gateway
- `default-request-channel`: This is the channel on which gateway puts the message for processing
- `default-reply-channel`: This is the channel on which gateway expects a reply

The interface is a simple Java interface declaration:

```
public interface FeedService {
  FeedEntitycreateFeed(FeedEntity feed);
  List<FeedEntity>readAllFeed();
}
```

We defined an interface and then defined the channels on which messages will be sent and read through using the gateway—but where is the implementation class that the components use to process the message and acknowledge it? Here, some Spring Integration magic is involved—when this XML is parsed, a proxy for this interface is created by the framework's `GatewayProxyFactoryBean` class. If there is a service request for a declared gateway, a proxy will forward the message on `default-request-channel` and will block the call until an acknowledgement is available on the `default-reply-channel`. The preceding declaration can be further extended to have channels per method call of the gateway:

```
<int:gateway id="feedService"
  service-interface="com.cpandey.siexample.service.FeedService"
  <int:method name="createFeed"
    request-channel="createFeedRequestChannel"/>
  <int:method name="readAllFeed"
    request-channel="readFeedRequestChannel"/>
</int:gateway>
```

Now when the `createFeed` method is called, messages will be put on `createFeedRequestChannel`, while for the `readAllFeed` method of gateway, messages will be forwarded to `readFeedRequestChannel`. Hold on a second—where is the `default-reply-channel`? The reply channel is an optional parameter and if it's not declared, an anonymous point-to-point reply channel is created by the gateway and is added to message headers with the name `replyChannel`. Explicit declaration would be helpful if we need a publish-subscribe channel to which multiple endpoints can listen.

We can easily leverage Spring Integration annotation support instead of using XML declarations:

```
public interface FeedService{
  @Gateway(requestChannel="createFeedRequestChannel")
    FeedEntitycreateFeed(FeedEntity feed);
  @Gateway(requestChannel="readFeedRequestChannel")
    List<FeedEntity>readAllFeed();
}
```

Asynchronous gateways

Asynchronous gateways do not expect an acknowledgement. After putting messages on the request channel, they move onto other processing without blocking for a reply on the reply channel. The Java language's `java.util.concurrent.Future` class provides a mechanism to fulfill this behavior; we can define our gateway service that returns a `Future` value. Let's modify `FeedService`:

```
public interface FeedService {
  Future<FeedEntity>createFeed(FeedEntity feed);
  Future<List<FeedEntity>>readAllFeed();
}
```

Nothing else changes and all XML declarations remain the same. When the return type is changed to `Future`, Spring framework's `GatewayProxyFactoryBean` class takes care of switching to asynchronous mode by leveraging `AsyncTaskExecutor`.

Service activators

Service activators are one of the simplest and most useful endpoints—a plain java class whose methods can be invoked on the messages received on a channel. Service activators can either terminate the message processing or pass it on to the next channel for further processing. Let's have a look at the following example. We would like to do some validation or business logic before passing the message on to the next channel. We can define a Java class and annotate it as follows:

```
@MessageEndpoint
public class PrintFeed {
  @ServiceActivator
  public String upperCase(String input) {
    //Do some business processing before passing the message
    return "Processed Message";
  }
}
```

In our XML, we can attach the class to a channel so that it processes each and every message on it:

```
<int:service-activator input-channel="printFeedChannel"
  ref="printFeed" output-channel="printFeedChannel" />
```

Let's quickly go through the elements used in the preceding declaration:

- `@MessageEndpoint`: This annotation tells Spring to treat a class as a specific Spring bean—a message endpoint. Since we have annotated this call with `MessageEndpoint`, there is no need to declare this bean in XML. It will be discovered in the component scan of Spring.

- `@ServiceActivator`: This annotation maps a method that should be invoked when a message arrives on the channel. This message is passed as a parameter.

- `int:service-activator`: This is an XML namespace declaring the Spring endpoint type.

- `input-channel`: This is the channel from which the service activator will read the messages.

- `output-channel`: This is the channel on which the activator will dump the processed messages.

- `ref`: This is a reference of the bean that performs the processing.

The preceding example restricts a single method in a class as `@ServiceActivator`. However, what if we want to delegate to an explicit method—maybe based on payloads? We define the method element for the service activator in the following code:

```
<int:service-activator ref="feedDaoService"
  method="printFeed" input-channel="printAllFeedChannel"/>

<int:service-activator ref="feedService" method="readFeed"
  input-channel="printAllFeedChannel"/>
```

In these two declarations, reference for the service activator is the same, that is, the class acting as the service is `feedDaoService`, but its different methods are invoked in different scenarios.

As we mentioned earlier, the output channel is optional. If the method return type is void, then it indicates that the message flow is terminated and Spring Integration is fine with it. However, what if the message type is not null and the output channel is also omitted? Spring Integration will try a fallback mechanism—it will try to look for a header with the name `replyChannel` in the message. If the value against the `replyChannel` header is of the type `MessageChannel`, then the messages will be sent to that channel. But if it's a string, then it will try looking for channels with that name. If both fail, then it will throw a `DestinationResolutionException` exception.

What type of message can a service activator process? The method argument can be either of the type `Message` or a Java `Object`. If it is `Message`, then we can read the payload and work upon it—but this introduces a dependency on the Spring `Message` type. A better approach is to declare the Java type as declared in the preceding example. Spring Integration will take care of extracting the payload and converting it to a declared object type before invoking the method on the service activator. If type conversion fails, an exception will be thrown. Similarly, returned data from the method is wrapped in a `Message` object and passed on to the next channel.

Can there be an activator method without any argument? Yes! This could be pretty useful in a scenario where we only care if an action was performed or not, for example, perhaps for an audit or for reporting purposes.

Delayers

As we already discussed in the introduction section, there could be a difference in the rate of messages produced and its rate of consumption—what if the consumer is slow? Since external systems are involved, it might not be in our control to influence the rate at which the producer produces messages. This is where a delayer is used. A **delayer** is a simple endpoint that introduces a delay before the message is delivered to the next endpoint. The most notable part is that the original sender is neither blocked nor slowed down; rather, the delayer will pick a message from a channel and use an instance of `org.springframework.scheduling.TaskScheduler` to schedule its delivery to the output channel after a configured interval. Let's write a simple delayer:

```
<int:delayer id="feedDelayer"
  input-channel="feedInput"
  default-delay="10000"
  output-channel="feedOutput"/>
```

This simple configuration will delay the delivery of messages on the input channel to the output channel by 10 seconds.

What if we want to delay each message with a different time interval—let's say based on payload size we want to increase or decrease the delay? The `expression` attribute comes in handy here. The preceding example can be modified as follows:

```
<int:delayer id="feedDelayer"
  input-channel="feedInput"
  default-delay="10000"
  output-channel="feedOutput"
  expression="headers['DELAY_MESSAGE_BY']"/>
```

Now each message can set a header name DELAY_MESSAGE_BY that will be used as an interval for delaying the message. If this header is not set, then default-delay will be used. Let's discuss each of the elements in the preceding configuration snippet:

- int:delayer: This is the Spring Integration namespace support for the delayer
- input-channel: This is the channel from which messages have to be delayed
- default-delay: This is the default delay duration in milliseconds
- output-channel: This is the channel where messages should be dropped after the delay is over
- expression: This is the expression that is evaluated to get the delay interval for each of the messages based on a set header value

The delayer delays message by certain intervals—what if the system goes down while there were delayed messages yet to be delivered on the output channel? We can leverage MessageStore, especially persistent MessageStore interfaces such as JdbcMessageStore. If it is used, then all messages are persisted as soon as the system goes down. When it comes up, all of the messages for which a delay interval has expired will be delivered on the output channel immediately.

Transactions

We have been talking about how message endpoints enable communication across different subsystems. This brings up a very crucial question—what about transactions? How are they handled across the chain? What are the Spring Integration offerings on transactions?

Spring Integration, per se, does not provide additional support for transactions; rather, it builds upon the existing infrastructure of the transaction support provided by Spring. It just provides hooks that can be used to plug in the transactional behavior. Annotating a service activator or gateway with a transactional annotation will support the transaction boundaries of the message flow. Let's say a user process was initiated with the transaction that is propagatory in nature and all Spring Integration components in the chain have been annotated as transactional, then a failure at any stage in the chain will result in a roll back. However, this will happen only if transaction boundaries have not been broken—put simply, everything is going on in a single thread. A single thread execution can break, for example, use cases such as task executor that spawns new threads, aggregators that can hold onto the messages, and time outs that can occur. Here is a quick example of making a poller transactional:

```
<int-jpa:inbound-channel-adapter
  channel="readFeedInfo"
  entity-manager="entityManager"
```

```
      auto-startup="true"
      jpa-query="select f from FeedDetailsf"
      <int:poller fixed-rate="2000" >
        <int:transactional propagation="REQUIRED"
          transaction-manager="transactionManager"/>
      </int:poller>
  </int-jpa:inbound-channel-adapter>
```

Here, `"entity-manager"`, `"transaction-manager"`, and so on are all standard Spring components—only the namespace from Spring Integration, such as `int-jpa` and `int:transactional`, has been used to plug them in. Right now, the adapter is of no interest to us; we will cover all other tags in subsequent chapters.

What about a use case where a process was not initiated with a transaction but, down the line, we want to introduce transactions on a subsystem? For example, a batch job or a poller that polls on a channel and picks a file to put it on an FTP server. There is no propagation of transactions, but we want to make this aspect transactional so that we can retry in case of failures. Spring Integration provides transaction support for pollers that can help start a transaction so that the process beyond a poller can be handled in a single unit of work! Here is a quick example:

```
  <int:poller max-messages-per-poll="1" fixed-rate="1000">
    <int:transactional transaction-manager="transactionManager"
      isolation="DEFAULT"
      propagation="REQUIRED"
      read-only="true"
      timeout="1000"/>
  </poller>
```

To summarize, Spring Integration hooks into the Spring transaction support and, with a little intuition and creativity, it can even be extended to systems that are nontransactional in nature!

Summary

In this chapter, we understood the reason why messaging endpoints are required, and discovered a few of the endpoints provided by Spring Integration. We covered how gateways can abstract underlying messaging implementation, making life simpler for a developer, how service activators can be used for intermediate processing of messages in the system, and how delayers can be used to throttle message processing rates to match the producer's and consumer's speed! We touched upon the transactional support—we discussed it only because it does not provide any new implementation and hooks into the Spring framework's transactional support.

In the next chapter, we will dive deeper into one of the most important endpoints—message transformers.

4
Message Transformers

The takeaway from the last chapter was that the message endpoints make the handshake transparent and seamless between two heterogeneous components. In this chapter, we will get into the details of one of the important concerns in integration—transformation of messages so that they can be consumed across a chain. We will cover:

- Message transformers
- Working with XML payload
- Enrichers
- Claim check

The same set of data can be viewed by different systems in different contexts, for example, an employee record is used by the reporting system as well as the finance system. However, the usage of the object will be different. Reporting systems just dump the employee record—so even if it gets it as a single string, it's okay. On the other hand, payroll systems might need to send mail notifications, calculate taxes based on state and country, and to carry out other functions for which employee data must be presented as a POJO, with information in a separate field, say, name, state, country, e-mail, and so on. Similarly, there could be cases where additional information must be augmented in the original message, it might be needed to encrypt/decrypt or to be converted to some proprietary format—these are the scenarios where message transformers make an entry!

Introducing message transformers

Message transformers are implementations of the **Enterprise Integration Pattern (EIP)** named **Message Translator**, which deal with parity between data formats across endpoints. It's a neat design to decouple message producers and message consumers — none of them are required to know the format expected by the other. It is almost like the adapter pattern from the core java design principle, which acts as an enabler across producers and consumers. Let's take a more generic example, we regularly transfer files across Windows and Linux even though the format required on these two systems is different, the underlying application takes care of transforming from one format to another.

Spring Integration provides a lot of out-of-the-box transformers without taking away flexibility to define and extend new transformers. It has provided extensive support for the most commonly used message exchange formats such as XML, JSON, Collections, and others. Out of these, by and large, XML is the most used language when it comes to cross-language and cross-platform communication. Let's take it up and explore Spring Integration support for XML before exploring other aspects of message transformation.

Working with XML payload

Two disparate systems might agree to interact via XML formats. This means that whenever there is an outgoing communication, the system's data structure needs to be converted to XML; while in the case of incoming messages, it needs to be converted to a data structure understood by the system. How do we do this? Spring provides first-class support to deal with XML via its **OXM (Object-to-XML)** framework. Marshalling and unmarshalling is done by classes — org.springframework. oxm.Marshaller and org.springframework.oxm.Unmarshaller, respectively. **Marshaller** converts an Object to an XML stream, while **unmarshaller** converts an XML stream to Object. Spring's Object/XML Mapping support provides several implementations supporting marshalling and unmarshalling using JAXB, Castor, and JiBX among others. Spring Integration abstracts it further and provides many out-of-the-box components, which help to deal with the XML payload. A few of them are *marshalling transformer*, *unmarshalling transformer*, and *XPath transformer*. There are many others such as Xslt transformer, XPath splitter, and XPath router but we will only cover the most used ones.

The marshalling transformer

A marshalling transformer is used to convert an object graph into an XML format. An optional result type can be provided, which can be a user-defined type, or one of the two Spring built-in types: `javax.xml.transform.dom.DOMResult` or `org.springframework.xml.transform.StringResult`.

Here is an example of a marshalling transformer:

```
<int-xml:marshalling-transformer
  input-channel="feedsMessageChannel"
  output-channel="feedXMLChannel"
  marshaller="marshaller"
  result-type="StringResult" />
```

An explanation of different elements used here is as follows:

- `int-xml:marshalling-transformer`: This is the namespace support provided by Spring Integration
- `input-channel`: This is the channel from which messages will be read
- `output-channel`: This is the channel on which transformed messages will be dropped
- `marshaller`: This is the marshaller instance to be used for marshalling
- `result-type`: This is the type to which results should be marshalled

A valid reference of the marshaller is required, for example:

```
<bean id="marshaller"
  class="org.springframework.oxm.castor.CastorMarshaller"/>
```

This example uses one of the Spring built-in types, `org.springframework.xml.transform.StringResult` as a result type. If `result-type` is not specified, then the default, `DOMResult`, is used. A custom result type can also be used here:

```
<int-xml:marshalling-transformer
  input-channel="feedsMessageChannel"
  output-channel="feedXMLChannel"
  marshaller="marshaller"
  result-factory="feedsXMLFactory"/>
```

Here, feedsXMLFactory refers to a class, which implements org.springframework.integration.xml.result.ResultFactor and overrides the method createResult:

```
public class FeedsXMLFactory implements ResultFactory {
  public Result createResult(Object payload) {
  //Do some stuff and return a type which implements
  //javax.xml.transform.result
  return //instance of javax.xml.transform.Result.
  }
}
```

The unmarshalling transformer

An unmarshalling transformer does the opposite of what the marshalling transformer does, that is, it takes an XML source and unmarshalls it. It requires an instance of source as a payload on a channel. If it finds a different payload, it tries out an automatic conversion. The String, File, and org.w3c.dom.Document payloads can be taken care of by Spring automagically. A custom conversion to Source can be provided by implementation of a source factory and its injection. The following code snippet is a simple example:

```
<int-xml:unmarshalling-transformer id="defaultUnmarshaller"
    input-channel=" feedsFile"
    output-channel="feedsMessage"
    unmarshaller="unmarshaller"/>
```

Almost all elements are the same as marshaller described earlier, except the unmarshaller element, which should point to a valid unmarshaller definition supported by Spring.

XPath transformers

Spring integration's xpath-transformer component can be used to parse an XML using XPath expressions:

```
<int-xml:xpath-transformer input-channel="feedsReadChannel"
    output-channel="feedTransformedChannel"
    xpath-expression="/feeds/@category" />
```

The XPath expression to be evaluated can be given using the tag xpath-expression. When an XML payload arrives on an input channel, the transformer parses the XPATH value and puts the result onto the output channel.

By default, the parsed value is converted to a message with a string payload but, if required, simple conversions can be done. The following implicit conversions are supported by Spring: BOOLEAN, DOM_OBJECT_MODEL, NODE, NODESET, NUMBER, and STRING. All of these are defined in javax.xml.xpath.XPathConstants, shown as follows:

```
<int-xml:xpath-transformer input-channel="feedsReadChannel"
   xpath-expression="/feeds/@category"
   evaluation-type=" STRING_RESULT"
   output-channel=" feedTransformedChannel "/>
```

The evaluation-type tag is used to introduce the desired conversion.

Validating XML messages

While we are discussing XML transformation, it's relevant to bring up the validation aspect of the XML payload. Prevalidation of XML will save the system from going in an erroneous condition and can act at the source. Spring Integration provides support for XML validation via a filter:

```
<int-xml:validating-filter
   id="feedXMLValidator"
   input-channel="feedsReadChannel"
   output-channel="feedsWriteChannel"
   discard-channel="invalidFeedReads"
   schema-location="classpath:xsd/feeds.xsd" />
```

The schema-location element defines the XSD that should be used for validation. This is optional and if it has not done so, set it to default xml-schema, which internally translates to org.springframework.xml. validation.XmlValidatorFactory#SCHEMA_W3C_XML.

We discussed a lot of inbuilt transformers, primarily dealing with XML payloads. Apart from these, Spring Integration provides many out-of-the-box transformers for the most common conversions, such as:

* object-to-string-transformer
* payload-serializing-transformer
* payload-deserializing-transformer
* object-to-map-transformer
* map-to-object-transformer
* json-to-object-transformer
* object-to-json-transformer and so on

Detailing each one is out of the scope of this book, but the concepts are the same as mentioned earlier.

Beyond default transformers

Spring does not restrict us to use the transformer provided by the framework, we can define our own transformer and it's pretty straightforward. All we need to do is to define a Java class, which takes a particular input type, coverts it to an expected format and puts it onto the output channel. Let's take an example where we want to convert our feed in a format that can be written to DB; we can define a class, which takes a *Message* payload of type com.sun.syndication.feed.synd.SyndEntry and converts it to com.cpandey.siexample.pojo.SoFeed, which is a JPA entity:

```
import com.cpandey.siexample.pojo.SoFeed;
import com.sun.syndication.feed.synd.SyndEntry;
public class SoFeedDbTransformer {
  publicSoFeedtransformFeed(Message<SyndEntry> message){
    SyndEntry entry = message.getPayload();
    SoFeed soFeed=new SoFeed();
    soFeed.setTitle(entry.getTitle());
    soFeed.setDescription(entry.getDescription().getValue());
    soFeed.setCategories(entry.getCategories());
    soFeed.setLink(entry.getLink());
    soFeed.setAuthor(entry.getAuthor());
    //For DB return soFeed
    returnsoFeed;
  }
```

A transformer can be declared using the following code:

```
<int:transformer ref="feedDbTransformerBean"
  input-channel="filteredFeedChannel"
  method="transformFeed"
  output-channel="jdbcChannel"/>
```

Let's take a quick look at the tags used in the preceding code snippet:

- int:transformer: This provides the XML namespace supported by Spring Integration
- ref: This is used to provide a reference of bean definition, which will act as the transformer
- input-channel: This is the channel from which messages will be picked up by the transformer

- `output-channel`: This is the channel where messages will be dropped after completing required transformations
- `method`: This is the method of the class that will have the transformation logic

Let's define the bean referred to by the `ref` tag:

```
<bean id="feedDbTransformerBean"
  class="com.cpandey.siexample.transformer.SoFeedDbTransformer" />
```

As explained earlier, this class has the required method for transformation. This bean can be used across transformers and each method can have separate transformation logic.

Content enrichers

While enabling interaction between heterogeneous systems, it might be necessary to augment the message with additional information so that it can be successfully processed by the next set of consumers. Let's take an example where in a batch processing environment, it might be necessary to attach priority information onto the incoming tasks. It is for a message that is put on a file server for external consumption—a timestamp indicating the max time for which the file would be kept should be added. There could be several such scenarios where the incoming message is incomplete and is to be processed by the next endpoint. Content enricher is a specialized form of transformer, which can attach additional information to the message. In the context of Spring Integration, the message consists of two parts—header and message payload. Spring Integration exposes a way to enrich either of these components.

Header enrichers

Header in Spring Integration is an instance of the `MessageHeaders` class, which in turn extends `Map<String,?>`. Headers are nothing but key-value pairs and their purpose is to provide metadata about the message. Adding an additional header is straightforward. Let's take an example, whenever feed arrives in our system and passes the XML validation, we will add a constant indicating that the feed is validated:

```
<int:header-enricher input-channel="validatedFeedsChannel"
  output-channel="nextChannelForProcess">
  <int:header name="validated" value="true"/>
</int:header-enricher>
```

Following is the description of the elements used in this code snippet:

- `int:header-enricher`: This element provides the Spring Integration XML namespace support for the header enricher
- `input-channel`: The header for each message on this channel will be enriched
- `output-channel`: Additional header messages will be dropped on this channel
- `int:header`: This is used to provide the key-value pair for the header name and header value

What if we want to add some dynamic value, let's say a timestamp, in a specific format? We can leverage bean support for the header enricher and define custom enrichment in the bean:

```
<int:header-enricher input-channel="feedsInputChannel"
  output-channel=" nextChannelForProcess ">
  <int:header name="customtimestamp"
    method="getTimeStamp"
    ref="timeStamp"/>
</int:header-enricher>
```

Where the bean referred to by the `ref` tag is as follows:

```
<bean id="timeStamp " class="com.cpandey.siexample.TimeStamp"/>
```

The definition of the actual class is as follows:

```
public class TimeStamp {
  public String getTimeStamp (String payload){
    return //a custom time stamp
  }
}
```

Apart from a standard Java Bean, we can also use a Groovy script to define the custom enricher:

```
<int:header-enricher input-channel="feedsInputChannel"
  output-channel=" nextChannelForProcess ">
  <int:header name="customtimestamp"
  <int-groovy:script location=""="siexample
    /TimeStampGroovyEnricher.groovy"/>
  </int:header>
</int:header-enricher>
```

There are predefined header elements that can also be used; the simplest and most commonly used is the error-channel:

```
<int:header-enricher input-channel=" feedsInputChannel "
  output-channel=" nextChannelForProcess ">
  <int:error-channel ref="feedserrorchannel"/>
</int:header-enricher>
```

Payload enrichers

Header enrichers are handy to add metadata information. What if the message itself is incomplete? Let's take an example, when a feed arrives, based on the feed category, it might be required to fetch metadata for that category, subscribed users for that category, and so on. Other components such as service activators and gateways can be used, but for ease of use Spring Integration has exposed payload enrichers. **Payload enrichers** are like gateways—they put messages onto a channel and then expect a reply for that message. The returned message will be payload enriched. For example, let's say external feeds have a lot of categories for Spring such as Spring-mvc, Spring-boot, Spring-roo, and Spring-data, but our system has a single category for all of these—Spring. Based on external categories, we can enrich the payload to use a single category:

```
<int:enricher id="consolidateCategoryEnricher"
  input-channel="findFeedCatoryChannel"
  request-channel="findInternalCategoryChannel">
  <int:property name="categroy"
    expression="payload.category"/>
  <int:property name="feedProcessed"
    value="true" type="java.lang.String"/>
</int:enricher>
```

Here, the configuration elements mean the following:

- `int:enricher`: This is used as Spring Integration namespace support for the enricher.
- `input-channel`: This is the channel from which data will be read for enrichment.
- `request-channel`: This is the channel to which data will be sent for enriching it.
- `int:property`: This is a convenient way to set the values on the target payload. The property mentioned must be "settable" on the target instance. It can be an **SpEL (Spring Expression Language)** expression, which is indicated by `expression` or it can be a value indicated by a value.

Claim check

We discussed the usage of header and content enrichers—they add additional information. However, in some circumstances, it might be a valid use case to hide the data—the simplest one can be a heavy payload. It's not a good idea to move the whole message around while most of the channels might be using just a subset or even just a pass-through! Enter a *claim check pattern*, which suggests storing data in accessible storage and then passing only the pointers around. Components that need the data to process can retrieve it using the pointer. Spring integration provides two components to accomplish this: *Incoming claim check transformer* and *Outgoing claim check transformer*. The incoming claim check transformer can be used to store the data while the outgoing one can be used to retrieve it.

Incoming claim check transformer

Incoming **claim check transformer** stores a message in the **message store** identified by its message-store tag, and transforms the payload to a pointer to the actual message, as can be seen in the following code snippet:

```
<int:claim-check-in id="feedpayloadin"
    input-channel="feedInChannel"
    message-store="feedMessageStore"
    output-channel="feedOutChannel"/>
```

Once the message is stored in the message store, it is indexed with a generated ID, which becomes a claim check for that message. The transformed message is the claim check, which is the new payload, and will be sent to the output channel. To retrieve this message, an outgoing claim check transformer is required.

Outgoing claim check transformer

The input channel for an outgoing claim check transformer must have a claim check as its payload, as shown in the following code snippet:

```
<int:claim-check-out id="feedpayloadout"
    input-channel="feedcheckoutChannel"
    message-store="feedMessageStore"
    output-channel="feedOutChannel"/>
```

Based on the claim check, this transformer converts the pointer back to the original payload and puts it back onto the output channel. What if we want to restrict the claim to once only? We can introduce a Boolean value for `remove-message`, setting its value to true will delete the message from the message store as soon as it has been claimed. The default value is false. The updated code is shown in the following code snippet:

```
<int:claim-check-out id="checkout"
  input-channel="checkoutChannel"
  message-store="testMessageStore"
  output-channel="output"
  remove-message="true"/>
```

Summary

We covered the ways in which a message can be enriched and transformed so that heterogeneous systems are decoupled from data formats of each other. We also covered the claim check concept, which is a special case of transformation and can be used for performance, security, and other nonfunctional aspects.

In the next chapter, we will move on to explore more out-of-the-box components provided by Spring Integration, which help with message flow.

5
Message Flow

We discussed message transformation in the last chapter. After transformation has been taken care of, there can be additional tasks before it can be delivered to the next in the chain. For example, messages might need some chunking, or they might be incomplete and need some temporary storage or sequencing. In this chapter, we will explore the out-of-the-box capabilities that the Spring Integration framework provides for a seamless flow of messages across heterogeneous components. We will cover the following topics in this chapter:

- Routers
- Filters
- Splitters
- Aggregators
- Resequencers
- Chaining handlers

Routers

Routers are components that pick messages from a channel and, depending on a set of pre-defined criteria, deliver them to different channels. Routers never change the message—they only route/reroute messages to the next destination. Spring Integration provides the following built-in routers:

- Payload-type router
- Header value router
- Recipient list router
- XPath router (part of the XML module)
- Error message exception-type router

Payload-type router

As the name suggests, this router will route the message based on the payload data type. For example, we can have a dedicated channel for string, another one for integer and yet another channel for a user-defined payload type. A simple code snippet from our feeds example is as follows:

```
<int:payload-type-router input-channel="transformedChannel">
  <int:mapping type="com.cpandey.siexample.pojo.SoFeed"
    channel="jdbcChannel" />
  <int:mapping type="java.lang.String" channel="jmsChannel" />
  <int:mapping type="org.springframework.messaging.Message"
    channel="mailChannel" />
</int:payload-type-router>
```

As can be observed from the preceding code snippet, depending on the payload type, the message is routed to different channels. The `java.lang.String` class has been configured to be routed to `jmsChannel`, while `org.springframework.messaging.Message` has been configured to be routed to `mailChannel`. The following two elements have been used:

- `int:payload-type-router`: This is used to provide a namespace for the payload-type router
- `int:mapping`: This is the tag used to provide mapping between the Java object and the channel

Header value router

Instead of using the type of message payload, this router will try to read headers that have been set on the payload:

```
<int:header-value-router
  input-channel="feedsChannel"
  header-name="feedtype">
  <int:mapping value="java" channel="javachannel" />
  <int:mapping value="spring" channel="springchannel" />
</int:header-value-router>
```

So, if the message payload contains a header named `feedtype`, then depending on its value, it can be routed to different channels. If the value is `java`, then it will be delivered to `javachannel`, while if its value is `spring`, then it will be delivered to `springchannel`.

This too has only two compulsory elements, namespace and mapping:

- `int:header-value-router`: This is the namespace for the class headervaluerouter.

- `int:mapping`: This is the element that maps the value of a header to the channel

The `mapping` keyword is optional, if it's not provided, the value of header, `header-name`, will be used to derive the channel name. For example, in the following code snippet, `mapping` has not been provided and hence the next channel will be `javachannel`, indicated by the `header-name` tag:

```
<int:header-value-router
   input-channel="feedsChannel"
   header-name="javachannel"/>
```

Recipient list router

Do not get confused with recipients who are users! Here, the recipient list refers to a list of channels, which can receive the message. It can be compared to the publish-subscribe channel use case, where a predefined set of channels are "subscribed" with the router:

```
<int:recipient-list-router input-channel="feedsChannel">
   <int:recipient channel="transformFeedChannel"/>
   <int:recipient channel="auditFeedChannel"/>
</int:recipient-list-router>
```

All the messages delivered on the feeds channel will be delivered both on `transformFeedChannel` and `auditFeedChannel`. The elements used are simple:

- `int:recipient-list-router`: This is used to provide a namespace for a recipientlist router

- `int:recipient`: This is used to provide the name of the channel, which should receive the message

XPath router

In *Chapter 4, Message Transformers*, we discussed handling XML payloads in detail and we discussed an example of *XPath*-based transformers. XPath router is similar — instead of transforming a message based on the XPath value, it is routed to one of the channels:

```
<int-xml:xpath-router input-channel="feedChannel">
   <int-xml:xpath-expression expression="/feed/type"/>
</int-xml:xpath-router>
```

This can send messages to a channel or a set of channels—the value of the expression will decide the channels to which messages should be routed. There is a way to route messages to specific channels based on the value of the expression:

```
<int-xml:xpath-router input-channel="feedChannel">
  <int-xml:xpath-expression expression="/feed/type"/>
  <int-xml:mapping value="java" channel="channelforjava"/>
  <int-xml:mapping value="spring" channel="channelforspring"/>
</int-xml:xpath-router>
```

Error message exception-type router

In the core Spring framework, we use exception mappers extensively. Error message exception-type router is an extension of the same concept. It can route messages to different channels based on the type of error or exception thrown while processing messages on the input channel. For example, in the following code snippet, if arguments are invalid, it will route to `invalidFeedChannel`, while for a `NullPointerException`, it will route to `npeFeedChannel`:

```
<int:exception-type-router
   input-channel="feedChannel"
   default-output-channel="defaultChannel">
<int:mapping
   exception-type="java.lang.IllegalArgumentException"
   channel="invalidFeedChannel"/>
 <int:mapping
    exception-type="java.lang.NullPointerException"
    channel="npeFeedChannel"/>
</int:exception-type-router>
<int:channel id=" illegalFeedChannel " />
<int:channel id=" npeFeedChannel " />
```

An explanation of the tags used in this code snippet is as follows:

- `int:exception-type-router`: This provides the namespace for exception-type router.

- `default-output-channel`: This is used to specify the default channel where the message should be delivered if none of the mappings can resolve a channel for the message. This is defined later in detail.

- `int:mapping exception-type`: This is used to map an exception to a channel name.

Default output channel

There can be cases where the router is unable to decide which channel a message should be delivered to—what to do in this case? The following two options are available:

- **Throw an exception**: Depending on a use case, this can be an exception that has been mapped to a channel, or the exception can be thrown to be propagated above in the chain.

- **Define a default output channel**: As the name suggests, this is the channel where all the messages for which channel delivery cannot be decided are delivered.

For example, in the preceding code snippet, the default channel has been specified as:

```
default-output-channel="defaultChannel"
```

If the exception cannot be mapped to a defined list, a message will be put on the default channel.

Using annotations

Spring's power comes from converting simple Java classes to specific components without extending or implementing external classes. To define routers, we can leverage the framework's @Router annotation. We can annotate any method with @Router, and can use its reference. Let's take an example where we want to route our feed based on the author:

```
@Component
public class AnnotatedFeedsAuthorRouter {
  @Router
  public String feedAuthor(Message<SoFeed > message) {
    SoFeed sf = message.getPayload();
    return sf.getAuthor() ;
  }
}
```

The return value is a string that is the author's name—a channel with the same name must be present. Alternatively, we can return MessageChannel or a list of MessageChannel references directly.

Filters

Message filters are Spring Integration components, which act as an interceptor and decide whether to pass on the message to the next channel/component or drop it. Unlike routers, which decide what should be the next channel for a message, filters only take a *boolean* decision—whether to pass or not. There are two ways to define a message filter in Spring Integration:

- Write a simple Java class and designate its method that will take decisions whether to pass the message or not

- Configure it as a message endpoint that delegates to an implementation of the `MessageSelector` interface

This can be configured either in XML or annotations can be used.

Using a Java class to act as a filter

Let's take an example of using a simple Java class as a filter—this is part of our example about feeds. As feeds come in, we try to validate whether the payload is empty or not—then only pass it on for further processing:

```
<int:filter
   input-channel="fetchedFeedChannel"
   output-channel="filteredFeedChannel"
   ref="filterSoFeedBean"
   method="filterFeed"/>
```

The tags interpretation is as simple and intuitive as it can be:

- `int:filter`: This is used to specify the Spring framework namespace for filters

- `input-channel`: This is the channel from which messages will be picked

- `output-channel`: This is the channel to which messages will be delivered if they pass the filtering criteria

- `ref`: This is used for the reference of the Java bean that is acting as a filter

- `method`: This is the method of the Java bean acting as a filter

Declaration for the bean acting as a filter is as follows:

```
<bean id="filterSoFeedBean"
class="com.cpandey.siexample.filter.SoFeedFilter"/>
```

An actual Java class that has method filtering for the messages, is shown in the following code snippet:

```
public class SoFeedFilter {
public boolean filterFeed(Message<SyndEntry> message){
  SyndEntry entry = message.getPayload();
  if(entry.getDescription()!=null&&entry.getTitle()!=null){
    return true;
  }
  return false;
}
}
```

We can also decide what to do if the payload fails the filtering criteria, for example, if the payload is empty. In such a case, we can do either of the following two options:

- An exception can be thrown
- It can be routed to a specific channel where action can be taken on it—say, just log the occurrence of a failure

To throw an exception, we can use the following code snippet:

```
<int:filter
    input-channel="fetchedFeedChannel"
    output-channel="filteredFeedChannel"
    ref="filterSoFeedBean"
    method="filterFeed"
    throw-exception-on-rejection="true"/>
```

To log the exception, we can use the following code snippet:

```
<int:filter
    input-channel="fetchedFeedChannel"
    output-channel="filteredFeedChannel"
    ref="filterSoFeedBean"
    method="filterFeed"
    discard-channel="rejectedFeeds"/>
```

Here, we used a filter on a direct channel and validated the payload. If validation was successful, we passed on the message; otherwise, we rejected the message either by throwing an exception or by logging its occurrence. Another use case for filters could be publish-subscribe channels—many endpoints can listen on a channel and filter out the messages of their interest.

We can also use *annotation* to define filters. Just using the `@Filter` annotation on a method of Java class and Spring Integration will convert it to a filter component — no need to extend or implement any additional reference:

```
@Component
public class SoFeedFilter {
  @Filter
  //Only process feeds which have value in its title and description
  public boolean filterFeed(Message<SyndEntry> message){
    SyndEntry entry = message.getPayload();
    if(entry.getDescription()!=null&&entry.getTitle()!=null){
      return true;
    }
    return false;
  }
}
```

A filter declaration in XML needs to be changed, no need to use the `method` parameter:

```
<int:filter
  input-channel="fetchedFeedChannel"
  output-channel="filteredFeedChannel"
  ref="filterSoFeedBean" />
```

Configuring a filter as a message endpoint

Another option to define a filter is to use frameworks (`MessageSelector`). The Java class needs to implement this interface and override the `accept` method. Whenever a payload is passed, the `accept` method is invoked and it returns a decision whether to pass on the message or drop it. The following code snippet modifies the previous example using `MessageSelector`:

```
public class SoFeedFilter implements MessageSelector{
public boolean accept(Message<?> message) {
    ...
    return true;
  }
  return false;
}
```

After this definition, the filter can be declared and used as follows:

```
<int:filter
  input-channel="fetchedFeedChannel"
  outputchannel="filteredFeedChannel">
  <bean class=" com.cpandey.siexample.filter.SoFeedFilter "/>
</int:filter>
```

Since bean class has been declared inline, there is no need for the reference tag.

Splitters

Splitters, as the name suggests, are used to split messages in smaller chunks and then send such resulting chunks for independent processing. There can be several reasons for splitting—larger size of payload than that of what is acceptable by the next endpoint, or message load parts that can be processed in parallel or down the chain. There is an aggregator and it is necessary to do some processing before these can be aggregated. Spring Integration provides a `splitter` tag. As in the case of a filter, splitters can also be written either by extending the framework interface or by writing a custom POJO.

Let's take the simpler one first, leveraging a simple Java class as a splitter:

```
<int:splitter
  ref="splitterSoFeedBean"
  method="splitAndPublish"
  input-channel="filteredFeedChannel"
  output-channel="splitFeedOutputChannel" />


<bean id="splitterSoFeedBean"
  class="com.cpandey.siexample.splitter.SoFeedSplitter"/>
```

The elements are pretty self-explanatory:

- `int:splitter`: This is used to specify the Spring framework namespace for filters
- `ref`: This is used to provide a reference of bean acting as a splitter
- `method`: This is used to specify a method in bean having message splitting implementation
- `input-channel`: This is the channel from which messages will be read
- `output-channel`: This is the channel on which messages will be written

Java class acting as a splitter:

```
public class SoFeedSplitter {
    public List<SyndCategoryImpl> plitAndPublish(Message<SyndEntry>
      message) {
    SyndEntry syndEntry=message.getPayload();
    List<SyndCategoryImpl> categories= syndEntry.getCategories();
    return categories;
    }
}
```

Splitters must return a type of collection, and each item from that collection is then delivered one at a time to the next endpoint. If the returned value is not a message type, then each element will be wrapped in a message type before delivery. Let's define a service activator for this splitter:

```
<int:service-activator
  id="splitChannelSA"
  ref="commonServiceActivator"
  method="printSplitMessage"
  input-channel="splitFeedOutputChannel"/>
```

The method `printSplitMessage` is defined in the following code snippet:

```
public void printSplitMessage(Message<SyndCategoryImpl> message) {
    if(message!=null){
      System.out.println(message.getPayload());
    }else{
      System.out.println("Message is null");
    }

}
```

We can avoid using the `method` tag by using annotation:

```
@Splitter
public List<SyndCategoryImpl> splitAndPublish(Message<SyndEntry>
message) {
    SyndEntry syndEntry=message.getPayload();
    List<SyndCategoryImpl> categories= syndEntry.getCategories();
    return categories;
}
```

As in the case of filters, we can also use framework support to write our splitters. Any Java class can extend `AbstractMessageSplitter` and override `splitMessage`. The previous example has been modified by extending the framework support in the following code snippet:

```
public class SoFeedSplitter extends AbstractMessageSplitter {
  @Override
  protected Object splitMessage(Message<?> message) {
    SyndEntry syndEntry=(SyndEntry)message.getPayload();
    List<SyndCategoryImpl> categories= syndEntry.getCategories();
    return categories;
  }
}
```

Aggregators

The aggregators are the opposite of splitters—they combine multiple messages and present them as a single message to the next endpoint. This is a very complex operation, so let's start by a real life scenario. A news channel might have many correspondents who can upload articles and related images. It might happen that the text of the articles arrives much sooner than the associated images—but the article must be sent for publishing only when all relevant images have also arrived. This scenario throws up a lot of challenges; partial articles should be stored somewhere, there should be a way to correlate incoming components with existing ones, and also there should be a way to identify the completion of a message. Aggregators are there to handle all of these aspects—some of the relevant concepts that are used are `MessageStore`, `CorrelationStrategy`, and `ReleaseStrategy`. Let's start with a code sample and then we will dive down to explore each of these concepts in detail:

```
<int:aggregator
  input-channel="fetchedFeedChannelForAggregatior"
  output-channel="aggregatedFeedChannel"
  ref="aggregatorSoFeedBean"
  method="aggregateAndPublish"
  release-strategy="sofeedCompletionStrategyBean"
  release-strategy-method="checkCompleteness"
  correlation-strategy="soFeedCorrelationStrategyBean"
  correlation-strategy-method="groupFeedsBasedOnCategory"
  message-store="feedsMySqlStore "
  expire-groups-upon-completion="true">
  <int:poller fixed-rate="1000"></int:poller>
</int:aggregator>
```

Hmm, a pretty big declaration! And why not—a lot of things combine together to act as an aggregator. Let's quickly glance at all the tags used:

- `int:aggregator`: This is used to specify the Spring framework's namespace for the aggregator.

- `input-channel`: This is the channel from which messages will be consumed.

- `output-channel`: This is the channel to which messages will be dropped after aggregation.

- `ref`: This is used to specify the bean having the method that is called on the release of messages.

- `method`: This is used to specify the method that is invoked when messages are released.

- `release-strategy`: This is used to specify the bean having the method that decides whether aggregation is complete or not.

- `release-strategy-method`: This is the method having the logic to check for completeness of the message.

- `correlation-strategy`: This is used to specify the bean having the method to correlate the messages.

- `correlation-strategy-method`: This is the method having the actual logic to correlate the messages.

- `message-store`: This is used to specify the message store, where messages are temporarily stored until they have been correlated and are ready to release. This can be in memory (which is default) or can be a persistence store. If a persistence store is configured, message delivery will be resumed across a server crash.

Java class can be defined as an aggregator and, as described in the previous bullet points, the `method` and `ref` parameters decide which method of bean (referred by `ref`) should be invoked when messages have been aggregated as per `CorrelationStrategy` and released after fulfilment of `ReleaseStrategy`. In the following example, we are just printing the messages before passing them on to the next consumer in the chain:

```
public class SoFeedAggregator {
  public List<SyndEntry> aggregateAndPublish(List<SyndEntry>
    messages) {
    //Do some pre-processing before passing on to next channel
    return messages;
  }
}
```

Let's get to the details of the three most important components that complete the aggregator.

Correlation strategy

Aggregator needs to group the messages—but how will it decide the groups? In simple words, `CorrelationStrategy` decides how to correlate the messages. The default is based on a header named `CORRELATION_ID`. All messages having the same value for the `CORRELATION_ID` header will be put in one bracket. Alternatively, we can designate any Java class and its method to define a custom correlation strategy or can extend Spring Integration framework's `CorrelationStrategy` interface to define it. If the `CorrelationStrategy` interface is implemented, then the `getCorrelationKey()` method should be implemented. Let's see our correlation strategy in the feeds example:

```
public class CorrelationStrategy {
  public Object groupFeedsBasedOnCategory(Message<?> message) {
    if(message!=null){
      SyndEntry entry = (SyndEntry)message.getPayload();
      List<SyndCategoryImpl> categories=entry.getCategories();
      if(categories!=null&&categories.size()>0){
        for (SyndCategoryImpl category: categories) {
          //for simplicity, lets consider the first category
          return category.getName();
        }
      }
    }
    return null;
  }
}
```

So how are we correlating our messages? We are correlating the feeds based on the category name. The method must return an object that can be used for correlating the messages. If a user-defined object is returned, it must satisfy the requirements for a key in a map such as defining `hashcode()` and `equals()`. The return value must not be null.

Alternatively, if we would have wanted to implement it by extending framework support, then it would have looked like this:

```
public class CorrelationStrategy implements CorrelationStrategy {
  public Object getCorrelationKey(Message<?> message) {
    if(message!=null){
      ...
            return category.getName();
```

```
            }
          }
        }
      return null;
    }
  }
}
```

Release strategy

We have been grouping messages based on correlation strategy – but when will we release it for the next component? This is decided by the release strategy. Similar to the correlation strategy, any Java POJO can define the release strategy or we can extend framework support. Here is the example of using the Java POJO class:

```
public class CompletionStrategy {
  public boolean checkCompleteness(List<SyndEntry> messages) {
    if (messages!=null){
      if (messages.size()>2){
        return true;
      }
    }
    return false;
  }
}
```

The argument of a message must be of type collection and it must return a Boolean indication whether to release the accumulated messages or not. For simplicity, we have just checked for the number of messages from the same category – if it's greater than two, we release the messages.

Message store

Until an aggregated message fulfils the release criteria, the aggregator needs to store them temporarily. This is where message stores come into the picture. Message stores can be of two types: in-memory and persistence store. Default is in memory, and if this is to be used, then there is no need to declare this attribute at all. If a persistent message store needs to be used, then it must be declared and its reference should be given to the message-store attribute. A mysql message store can be declared and referenced as follows:

```
<bean id=" feedsMySqlStore "
  class="org.springframework.integration.jdbc.JdbcMessageStore">
  <property name="dataSource" ref="feedsSqlDataSource"/>
</bean>
```

Data source is Spring framework's standard JDBC data source. The greatest advantage of using persistence store is recoverability—if the system recovers from a crash, all in-memory aggregated messages will not be lost. Another advantage is capacity—memory is limited, which can accommodate a limited number of messages for aggregation, but the database can have a much bigger space.

Resequencers

A **resequencer** can be used to enforce an ordered delivery to the next subsystem. It will hold on to a message till all messages numbered before it have been delivered. For example, if messages have been numbered 1 to 10 and if the message numbered 8 arrives sooner than the messages numbered 1 to 7, it will hold it in temporary storage and will be delivered only when the delivery of messages numbered 1 to 7 is complete. The SEQUENCE_NUMBER header of the message is used by resequencer to track the sequences. It can be considered as a special case of aggregator, which holds on to the message based on a header value but does not do any processing on the messages:

```
<int:resequencer input-channel="fetchedFeedChannelForAggregatior"
  output-channel="cahinedInputFeedChannel"
  release-strategy="sofeedResCompletionStrategyBean"
  release-strategy-method="checkCompleteness"
  correlation-strategy="soFeedResCorrelationStrategyBean"
  correlation-strategy-method="groupFeedsBasedOnPublishDate"
  message-store="messageStore">
  <int:poller fixed-rate="1000"></int:poller>
</int:resequencer >
```

As we mentioned, resequencers can be considered as a special case of aggregators—almost all tags mean the same, except the namespace declaration.

Chaining handlers

We have discussed quite a lot of handlers provided by Spring Integration as filters, transformers, service activators, and so on, which can be independently applied on to the message—Spring Integration further provides a mechanism to chain these handlers. A special implementation of MessageHandler is MessageHandlerChain, can be configured as a single message endpoint. It is a chain of other handlers, and a message received simply delegates it to the configured handlers in a predefined sequence. Let's take an example:

```
<int:chain
  input-channel="cahinedInputFeedChannel"
  output-channel="logChannel">
```

```
    input-channel="cahinedInputFeedChannel"
    output-channel="logChannel">
    <int:filter ref="filterSoFeedBean"
      method="filterFeed"
      throw-exception-on-rejection="true"/>
    <int:header-enricher>
      <int:header name="test" value="value"/>
    </int:header-enricher>
    <int:service-activator
      ref="commonServiceActivator"
      method="chainedFeed"/>
  </int:chain>
```

Let's quickly create a chain and validate it. Start with a filter, which just passes all the messages, add a header in the next step, and finally print the headers in the service activator. If we can confirm the existence of added headers in the second step, then we are fine — chain executed!

Summary

Let's take a deep breath… This has been a long chapter and we covered many out-of-the-box components provided by the Spring Integration framework such as routers, filters, and splitters. These all helped with message flow across different endpoints. In the next chapter, we will continue exploring Spring Integration framework's out-of-the-box capabilities, but the focus will be more on adapters to interact with external systems such as connecting to a database, fetching tweets from Twitter, writing to a JMS queue, interacting with an FTP server, and many more — a lot of interesting stuff, stay tuned!

6
Integration with External Systems

In the previous chapter, we discussed Spring Integration components that help with message flow inside systems. In this chapter, let's pull the lever further and see what Spring Integration has in the box when it comes to real-world integration challenges. We will cover Spring Integration's support for external components and we will cover the following topics in detail:

- Working with files
- File exchange over FTP/FTPS
- Social integration
- Enterprise messaging
- Invoking and consuming HTTP endpoints
- Web services
- Database integration
- Streaming

Working with files

One of the most common and primitive ways to communicate is through files. Even after the introduction of databases, the filesystem has not lost its relevance and we frequently need to deal with them — in legacy applications, for dumping reports, shared locations, and so on.

So, how do you work with files in Java? Get the file handle, open a stream, work over it, and then close it. Some trivial stuff would take 10-15 lines of code. However, what if you forget to close the stream or the referenced file has been removed? The lines of code go on increasing as we handle all the corner cases. Spring Integration has very good support for files. It provides adapters and gateways that can handle file reading and writing operations with minimal lines of code.

Prerequisites

To use the file components mentioned previously, we need to declare the Spring namespace support and Maven entry in the following way:

- Namespace support can be added by using the following code snippet:

```
xmlns:int-file
  ="http://www.springframework.org/schema/integration/file"
xsi:schemaLocation=
"http://www.springframework.org/schema/integration/file
http://www.springframework.org/schema/integration/file/spring-
integration-file.xsd">
```

- Maven entry can be added by using the following code snippet:

```
<dependency>
    <groupId>org.springframework.integration</groupId>
    <artifactId>spring-integration-file</artifactId>
    <version>${spring.integration.version}</version>
</dependency>
```

We are now good to start writing our Spring Integration file components. Let's discuss file support from Spring based on the two types of operation: reading files and writing files.

Reading files

Spring Integration provides an adapter that can read a file from a directory and make it available as a `Message<File>` on a channel for other consumers to consume it. Let's look at a snippet to see how it is configured:

```
<int-file:inbound-channel-adapter
  id="fileAdapter"
  directory="C:\Chandan\Projects\inputfolderforsi"
  channel="filesOutputChannel"
  prevent-duplicates="true"
  filename-pattern="*.txt">
```

```
    <int:poller fixed-rate="1000" />
    <int-file:nio-locker/>
</int-file:inbound-channel-adapter>
```

The preceding configuration is sufficient to read files from a *directory* and put it on the specified *channel*. Let's look at the elements:

- `int-file:inbound-channel-adapter`: This is the namespace for file support
- `directory`: This is the directory from where files should be read
- `channel`: This is the channel on which a file should be written
- `prevent-duplicates`: If this is enabled, files already picked up in an earlier run are not picked up again
- `filename-pattern`: This is the name pattern for the file that should be picked up
- `int:poller`: This is the rate at which files should be polled
- `int-file:nio-locker`: If there are multiple consumers, this will lock files so that the same files are not picked concurrently

You must have realized that although the configuration is simple, a lot of things are going on under the hood, such as preventing duplicates, filtering files, avoiding concurrent access, and so on. We will discuss these in detail, but before that let's have a peek at the class that is acting behind the scene for this adapter.

Behind the scenes

The adapter declared in the previous example leverages `FileReadingMessageSource`, which is an implementation of `MessageSource`. It creates a message based on a file from a directory as follows:

```
<bean
  id="pollableFileSource"
  class="org.springframework.integration.file.
    FileReadingMessageSource"
  p:directory="C:\Chandan\Projects\inputfolderforsi" />
```

At bean declaration level, we can inject filters, locking mechanics, and so on—but since we are using Spring Integration, it spares us from working at bean declaration level. Instead, we can use adapters exposed by Spring Integration.

Filters

Filter is a powerful concept that can be used to prevent duplicates, select files based on name patterns, customize the list of files read, and perform many more interceptions before the required content can be presented to the next endpoint. There are predefined filters available for most common tasks, but in the true spirit of spring, we can have custom implementations as well and inject them in adapters provided by Spring Integration. Filters must be an instance of `FileListFilter`, and the default filter used is `AcceptOnceFileListFilter`. This filter keeps track of processed files, but the implementation is in-memory. This means that if the server restarts when files are being processed, it will lose track of which files have been processed and will re-read the same files. To overcome this issue, an instance of `FileSystemPersistentAcceptOnceFileListFilter` should be used, which will keep track of processed files by leveraging the `MetadataStore` implementation.

Additionally, filename patterns and `Reg Ex` filters are available and can be used to filter files based on their names or by matching the name against the `Reg Ex` specified. Let's see a quick example showing the use of these two filters:

```
<int-file:inbound-channel-adapter
  id="filestest1"
  directory="file:${input.directory}"
  filename-pattern="testing*" />

<int-file:inbound-channel-adapter
  id="filestest2"
  directory="file:${input.directory}"
  filename-regex="testing[0-9]+\.jpg" />
```

Let's say we want a custom filter, it can easily be defined and used. The code is as follows:

```
public class CustomFilter implements FileListFilter<Feed> {
  public List< Feed > filterFiles(Feed [] feeds) {
    List< Feed > filteredList = new ArrayList< Feed >();
    // implement your filtering logic here
    return filteredList;
  }
}
```

Preventing duplicates

Preventing duplicates is a subset of filter that filters out files that have already been picked up. Using `prevent-duplicates`, we can instruct an adapter to look for unique files only. The only glitch here is that a duplicate check is limited to a session, as the reader does not store any state. If the reader restarts, it will read all the files again—even though they have been read earlier.

Concurrent access

This is a very common use case in enterprises with multiple consumers, and we want to maintain the sanity of the files consumed. We can use the `java.nio` locker in the following way to lock files to ensure that they are not accessed concurrently:

```
<int-file:inbound-channel-adapter
  id="fileReader"
  directory="C:\Chandan\Projects\inputfolderforsi"
  prevent-duplicates="true">
    <int-file:nio-locker/>
</int-file:inbound-channel-adapter>
```

This code does not restrict us to use only `java.nio.locker`. Instead of using the `java.nio` locker, we can provide custom lockers as well:

```
<int-file:inbound-channel-adapter
  id="fileAdapter"
  directory="C:\Chandan\Projects\inputfolderforsi"
  prevent-duplicates="true">
  <int-file:locker ref="customLocker"/>
</int-file:inbound-channel-adapter>
```

 Unlocking is not explicit. It is performed by calling `FileLocker.unlock(File file);` otherwise, it will result in memory leaks over the period.

Writing files

Spring Integration provides outbound adapters, which are the opposite of inbound adapters. This means that it consumes a file from a channel and writes it to a directory. Internally, Spring Integration uses an instance of `FileWritingMessageHandler` to write messages to the filesystem, and an implementation of this class can be used. This class can deal with files, strings, or byte array payloads. As usual, there is no need to use the low-level classes; instead, adapter and gateway exposed by spring can be used. Let's connect an outbound adapter to the channel on which the inbound adapter writes files:

```
<int-file:outbound-channel-adapter
  channel="filesOutputChannel"
  directory="C:\Chandan\Projects\outputfolderforsi"
  delete-source-files="true"/>
```

Let's discuss what each element represents:

- `int-file:outbound-channel-adapter`: This provides file namespace support for the outbound channel adapter
- `channel`: This is the channel where the files would be written as Spring Integration messages
- `directory`: This is the directory from which files are picked
- `delete-source-files`: If this is set to true, it will delete the files after processing them

While writing files, we need to consider things such as what should be the name of the new file, which directory should it be written in, what should be done with the original file, and so on. Let's quickly touch upon these aspects.

Naming the file

By default, the name of the file will be retained when it is written in the directory. However, this can be overridden by providing an implementation `FileNameGenerator`. This is the class responsible for generating the filenames — by default `FileNameGenerator` looks for a message header whose key matches the constant `FileHeaders.FILENAME`.

Target directory

There are primarily three ways to locate the target directory:

- Statically define a directory attribute that will direct each message to a fixed directory.
- Define a directory-expression attribute that should be a valid **Spring Expression Language (SpEL)** expression. This expression is evaluated for each message and the message header can be used to dynamically specify the output file directory. The expression must resolve to a string or to `java.io.File`, and this must point to a valid directory.
- The last option is the auto create directory. If the destination directory is missing, it will be created automatically, including its parent directory. This is the default behavior; to disable this, set the `auto-create-directory` attribute to `false`.

Dealing with existing filenames

What if the file being written already exists? The correct route to take is using the `mode` attribute. One of following four options is available:

- `REPLACE`: This is the default mode. If a file already exists, it will be simply overwritten.

- `APPEND`: This will append the content of the incoming file to the existing one.

- `FAIL`: If a duplicate is not expected, this mode should be used. This will throw `MessageHandlingException` if the file already exists.

- `IGNORE`: If no action needs to be taken if the target file exists, this option should be used.

So far, we have covered most of the aspects of the filesystem. However, what if we want to process the message after it has been written to the directory? Spring Integration provides an outbound gateway that can be handy here. Let's have a look at this simple example:

```
<int-file:outbound-gateway
    request-channel="filesOutputChannel"
    reply-channel="filesOutputChannelGateway"
    directory="C:\Chandan\Projects\outputfolderforsi\filegateway"
    mode="REPLACE" delete-source-files="true"/>
```

The tags are the same as those for the output adapter; the difference is that it puts the files on the channel specified by `reply-channel` for further processing.

Let's write a simple service activator that will process these files:

```
<int:service-activator
    id="fileSa"
    ref="commonServiceActivator"
    method="printFileName" input-channel="filesOutputChannelGateway"/>
```

File transformers

File transformers are used to transform data read from a file to an object and vice versa. Spring Integration has provided a few common transformers such as file to byte, file to string, and so on, but we can always extend the framework interfaces to define more advanced and appropriate file transformers.

Let's complete this section with a quick discussion on some implicit file transformers provided by spring. Let's start with this example:

```
<int-file:file-to-bytes-transformer
   input-channel="input"
   output-channel="output"
   delete-files="true"/>

<int-file:file-to-string-transformer
   input-channel="input"
   output-channel="output"
   delete-files="true"
   charset="UTF-8"/>
```

As it's obvious from the preceding snippet, Spring Integration has provided implicit transformers for most common use cases as file to byte and file to string. Transformers are not restricted to these two cases—custom transformers can be defined by implementing the transformer interface or extending `AbstractFilePayloadTransformer`.

FTP/FTPS

FTP, or **File Transfer Protocol**, is used to transfer files across networks. FTP communications consist of two parts: server and client. The client establishes a session with the server, after which it can download or upload files. Spring Integration provides components that act as a client and connect to the FTP server to communicate with it. What about the server—which server will it connect to? If you have access to any public or hosted FTP server, use it. Else, the easiest way for trying out the example in this section is to set up a local instance of the FTP server. FTP setup is out of the scope of this book.

Prerequisites

To use Spring Integration components for FTP/FTPS, we need to add a namespace to our configuration file and then add the Maven dependency entry in the `pom.xml` file. The following entries should be made:

- Namespace support can be added by using the following code snippet:

```
xmlns:int-ftp=
   "http://www.springframework.org/schema/integration/ftp"
xsi:schemaLocation=
   "http://www.springframework.org/schema/integration/ftp
   http://www.springframework.org/schema/integration/ftp/spring-
   integration-ftp.xsd"
```

- Maven entry can be added by using the following code snippet:

```
<dependency>
  <groupId>org.springframework.integration</groupId>
  <artifactId>spring-integration-ftp</artifactId>
  <version>${spring.integration.version}</version>
</dependency>
```

Once namespace is available and the JAR has been downloaded, we are ready to use the components. As mentioned earlier, client components of Spring Integration need a session to establish with the FTP server. The details of the session is encapsulated in the session factory; let's look at a sample session factory configuration:

```
<bean id="ftpClientSessionFactory"
  class="org.springframework.integration.
    ftp.session.DefaultFtpSessionFactory">
  <property name="host" value="localhost"/>
  <property name="port" value="21"/>
  <property name="username" value="testuser"/>
  <property name="password" value="testuser"/>
</bean>
```

The `DefaultFtpSessionFactory` class is at work here, and it takes the following parameters:

- Host that is running the FTP server
- Port at which it's running the server
- Username
- Password for the server

A session pool for the factory is maintained and an instance is returned when required. Spring takes care of validating that a stale session is never returned.

Downloading files from the FTP server

Inbound adapters can be used to read the files from the server. The most important aspect is the session factory that we just discussed in the preceding section. The following code snippet configures an FTP inbound adapter that downloads a file from a remote directory and makes it available for processing:

```
<int-ftp:inbound-channel-adapter
  channel="ftpOutputChannel"
  session-factory="ftpClientSessionFactory"
  remote-directory="/"
```

```
    local-directory=
    "C:\\Chandan\\Projects\\siexample\\ftp\\ftplocalfolder"
    auto-create-local-directory="true"
    delete-remote-files="true"
    filename-pattern="*.txt"
    local-filename-generator-expression=
    "#this.toLowerCase() + '.trns'">
    <int:poller fixed-rate="1000"/>
</int-ftp:inbound-channel-adapter>
```

Let's quickly go through the tags used in this code:

- `int-ftp:inbound-channel-adapter`: This is the namespace support for the FTP inbound adapter.

- `channel`: This is the channel on which the downloaded files will be put as a message.

- `session-factory`: This is a factory instance that encapsulates details for connecting to a server.

- `remote-directory`: This is the directory on the server where the adapter should listen for the new arrival of files.

- `local-directory`: This is the local directory where the downloaded files should be dumped.

- `auto-create-local-directory`: If enabled, this will create the local directory structure if it's missing.

- `delete-remote-files`: If enabled, this will delete the files on the remote directory after it has been downloaded successfully. This will help in avoiding duplicate processing.

- `filename-pattern`: This can be used as a filter, but only files matching the specified pattern will be downloaded.

- `local-filename-generator-expression`: This can be used to generate a local filename.

An inbound adapter is a special listener that listens for events on the remote directory, for example, an event fired on the creation of a new file. At this point, it will initiate the file transfer. It creates a payload of type `Message<File>` and puts it on the output channel. By default, the filename is retained and a file with the same name as the remote file is created in the local directory. This can be overridden by using `local-filename-generator-expression`.

Incomplete files

On the remote server, there could be files that are still in the process of being written. Typically, there the extension is different, for example, `filename.actualext.writing`. The best way to avoid reading incomplete files is to use the filename pattern that will copy only those files that have been written completely.

Uploading files to the FTP server

Outbound adapters can be used to write files to the server. The following code snippet reads a message from a specified channel and writes it inside the FTP server's remote directory. The remote server session is determined as usual by the session factory. Make sure the username configured in the session object has the necessary permission to write to the remote directory. The following configuration sets up a FTP adapter that can upload files in the specified directory:

```
<int-ftp:outbound-channel-adapter channel="ftpOutputChannel"
  remote-directory="/uploadfolder"
  session-factory="ftpClientSessionFactory"
  auto-create-directory="true">
</int-ftp:outbound-channel-adapter>
```

Here is a brief description of the tags used:

- `int-ftp:outbound-channel-adapter`: This is the namespace support for the FTP outbound adapter.
- `channel`: This is the name of the channel whose payload will be written to the remote server.
- `remote-directory`: This is the remote directory where files will be put. The user configured in the session factory must have appropriate permission.
- `session-factory`: This encapsulates details for connecting to the FTP server.
- `auto-create-directory`: If enabled, this will automatically create a remote directory if it's missing, and the given user should have sufficient permission.

The payload on the channel need not necessarily be a file type; it can be one of the following:

- `java.io.File`: A Java file object
- `byte[]`: This is a byte array that represents the file contents
- `java.lang.String`: This is the text that represents the file contents

Avoiding partially written files

Files on the remote server must be made available only when they have been written completely and not when they are still partial. Spring uses a mechanism of writing the files to a temporary location and its availability is published only when it has been completely written. By default, the suffix is written, but it can be changed using the `temporary-file`-suffix property. This can be completely disabled by setting `use-temporary-file-name` to `false`.

FTP outbound gateway

Gateway, by definition, is a two-way component: it accepts input and provides a result for further processing. So what is the input and output in the case of FTP? It issues commands to the FTP server and returns the result of the command. The following command will issue an `ls` command with the option `-1` to the server. The result is a list of string objects containing the filename of each file that will be put on the `reply-channel`. The code is as follows:

```
<int-ftp:outbound-gateway id="ftpGateway"
    session-factory="ftpClientSessionFactory"
    request-channel="commandInChannel"
    command="ls"
    command-options="-1"
    reply-channel="commandOutChannel"/>
```

The tags are pretty simple:

- `int-ftp:outbound-gateway`: This is the namespace support for the FTP outbound gateway
- `session-factory`: This is the wrapper for details needed to connect to the FTP server
- `command`: This is the command to be issued
- `command-options`: This is the option for the command
- `reply-channel`: This is the response of the command that is put on this channel

FTPS support

For FTPS support, all that is needed is to change the factory class — an instance of `org.springframework.integration.ftp.session.DefaultFtpsSessionFactory` should be used. Note the s in `DefaultFtpsSessionFactory`. Once the session is created with this factory, it's ready to communicate over a secure channel. Here is an example of a secure session factory configuration:

```
<bean id="ftpSClientFactory"
  class="org.springframework.integration.ftp.session.
  DefaultFtpsSessionFactory">
  <property name="host" value="localhost"/>
  <property name="port" value="22"/>
  <property name="username" value="testuser"/>
  <property name="password" value="testuser"/>
</bean>
```

Although it is obvious, I would remind you that the FTP server must be configured to support a secure connection and open the appropriate *port*.

Social integration

Any application in today's context is incomplete if it does not provide support for social messaging. Spring Integration provides in-built support for many social interfaces such as e-mails, Twitter feeds, and so on. Let's discuss the implementation of Twitter in this section. Prior to Version 2.1, Spring Integration was dependent on the Twitter4J API for Twitter support, but now it leverages Spring's social module for Twitter integration. Spring Integration provides an interface for receiving and sending tweets as well as searching and publishing the search results in messages. Twitter uses `oauth` for authentication purposes. An app must be registered before we start Twitter development on it.

Prerequisites

Let's look at the steps that need to be completed before we can use a Twitter component in our Spring Integration example:

- **Twitter account setup:** A Twitter account is needed. Perform the following steps to get the keys that will allow the user to use Twitter using the API:

    1. Visit `https://apps.twitter.com/`.
    2. Sign in to your account.

3. Click on **Create New App**.

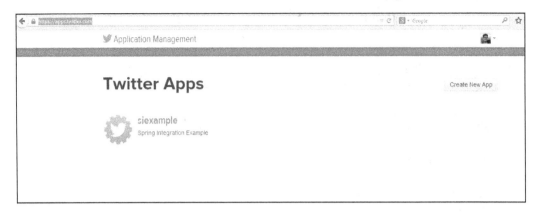

4. Enter the details such as **Application name**, **Description**, **Website**, and so on. All fields are self-explanatory and appropriate help has also been provided. The value for the field **Website** need not be a valid one — put an arbitrary website name in the correct format.

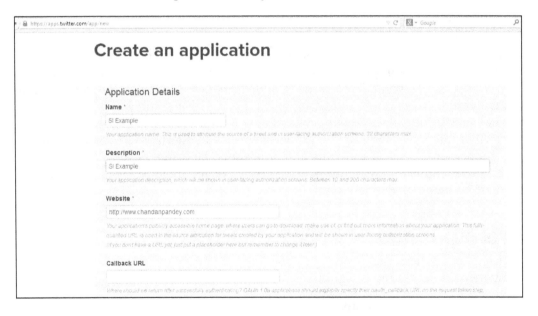

5. Click on the **Create your application** button. If the application is created successfully, a confirmation message will be shown and the **Application Management** page will appear, as shown here:

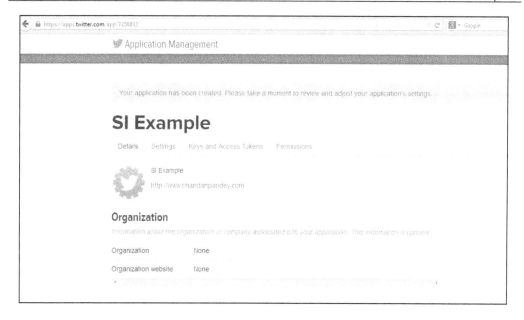

6. Go to the **Keys and Access Tokens** tab and note the details for **Consumer Key (API Key)** and **Consumer Secret (API Secret)** under **Application Settings**, as shown in the following screenshot:

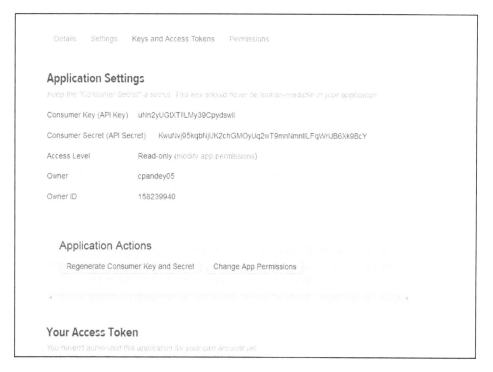

7. You need additional access tokens so that applications can use Twitter using APIs. Click on **Create my access token**; it takes a while to generate these tokens. Once it is generated, note down the value of **Access Token** and **Access Token Secret**.

8. Go to the **Permissions** tab and provide permission to **Read, Write and Access direct messages**.

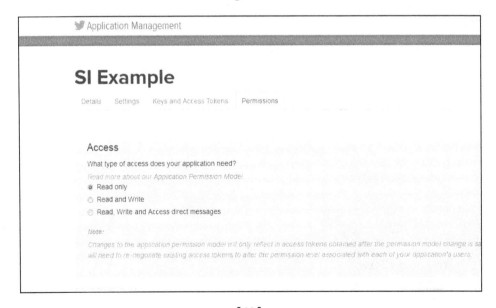

After performing all these steps, and with the required keys and access token, we are ready to use Twitter. Let's store these in the `twitterauth.` `properties` property file:

`twitter.oauth.apiKey``= lnrDlMXSDnJumKLFRym02kHsy`

`twitter.oauth.apiSecret``=`
`6wlriIX9ay6w2f6at6XGQ7oNugk6dqNQEAArTsFsAU6RU8F2Td`

`twitter.oauth.accessToken``=`
`158239940-FGZHcbIDtdEqkIA77HPcv3uosfFRnUM30hRix9TI`

`twitter.oauth.accessTokenSecret``=`
`H1oIeiQOlvCtJUiAZaachDEbLRq5m91IbP4bhg1QPRDeh`

The next step towards Twitter integration is the creation of a Twitter template. This is similar to the datasource or connection factory for databases, JMS, and so on. It encapsulates details to connect to a social platform. Here is the code snippet:

```
<context:property-placeholder location="classpath: twitterauth.
properties "/>

<bean id="twitterTemplate" class=" org.springframework.social.
  twitter.api.impl.TwitterTemplate ">
  <constructor-arg value="${twitter.oauth.apiKey}"/>
  <constructor-arg value="${twitter.oauth.apiSecret}"/>
  <constructor-arg value="${twitter.oauth.accessToken}"/>
  <constructor-arg value="${twitter.oauth.accessTokenSecret}"/>
</bean>
```

As I mentioned, the template encapsulates all the values. Here is the order of the arguments:

- `apiKey`
- `apiSecret`
- `accessToken`
- `accessTokenSecret`

With all the setup in place, let's now do some real work:

- Namespace support can be added by using the following code snippet:

```
<beans xmlns=
  "http://www.springframework.org/schema/beans"
  xmlns:xsi=
  "http://www.w3.org/2001/XMLSchema-instance"
  xmlns:int=
  "http://www.springframework.org/schema/integration"
```

```
xmlns:int-twitter=
"http://www.springframework.org/schema/integration/twitter"
xsi:schemaLocation=
"http://www.springframework.org/schema/integration http://www.
springframework.org/schema/integration/spring-integration.xsd
http://www.springframework.org/schema/beans http://www.
springframework.org/schema/beans/spring-beans.xsd
http://www.springframework.org/schema/integration/twitter
http://www.springframework.org/schema/integration/twitter/
spring-integration-twitter.xsd">
```

- Maven entry can be added by using the following code snippet:

```
<dependency>
  <groupId>org.springframework.integration</groupId>
  <artifactId>spring-integration-twitter</artifactId>
  <version>${spring.integration.version}</version>
</dependency>
```

Receiving tweets

Spring Integration has exposed inbound adapters for receiving tweets. Twitter tweets are of different types, and Spring provides support for receiving tweets as Timeline Updates, Direct Messages, Mention Messages, as well as Search Results.

Spring's inbound adapter is a polling-based mechanism that polls the Twitter site for updates at defined intervals. Be aware of Twitter's Rate Limiting; it limits the rate at which an application can poll for the updates. Factor this when setting the polling interval so that it's in compliance with the Twitter policies. Let's look at a working code snippet:

```
<int-twitter:inbound-channel-adapter id="testTweet"
  twitter-template="twitterTemplate"
  channel="twitterChannel">
</int-twitter:inbound-channel-adapter>
```

The components in this code are covered in the following bullet points:

- `int-twitter:inbound-channel-adapter`: This is the namespace support for Twitter's inbound channel adapter.
- `twitter-template`: This is the most important aspect. The Twitter template encapsulates which account to use to poll the Twitter site. The details given in the preceding code snippet are fake; it should be replaced with real connection parameters.
- `channel`: Messages are dumped on this channel.

These adapters are further used for other applications, such as for searching messages, retrieving direct messages, and retrieving tweets that mention your account, and so on. Let's have a quick look at the code snippets for these adapters. I will not go into detail for each one; they are almost similar to what have been discussed previously.

- **Search**: This adapter helps to search the tweets for the parameter configured in the query tag. The code is as follows:

```
<int-twitter:search-inbound-channel-adapter id="testSearch"
  twitter-template="twitterTemplate"
  query="#springintegration"
  channel="twitterSearchChannel">
</int-twitter:search-inbound-channel-adapter>
```

- **Retrieving Direct Messages**: This adapter allows us to receive the direct message for the account in use (account configured in Twitter template). The code is as follows:

```
<int-twitter:dm-inbound-channel-adapter
  id="testdirectMessage"
  twitter-template="twiterTemplate"
  channel="twitterDirectMessageChannel">
</int-twitter:dm-inbound-channel-adapter>
```

- **Retrieving Mention Messages**: This adapter allows us to receive messages that mention the configured account via the `@user` tag (account configured in the Twitter template). The code is as follows:

```
<int-twitter:mentions-inbound-channel-adapter
  id="testmentionMessage"
  twitter-template="twiterTemplate"
  channel="twitterMentionMessageChannel">
</int-twitter:mentions-inbound-channel-adapter>
```

Sending tweets

Twitter exposes outbound adapters to send messages. Here is a sample code:

```
<int-twitter:outbound-channel-adapter
  twitter-template="twitterTemplate"
  channel="twitterSendMessageChannel"/>
```

Whatever message is put on the `twitterSendMessageChannel` channel is tweeted by this adapter. Similar to an inbound gateway, the outbound gateway provides support for sending direct messages. Here is a simple example of an outbound adapter:

```
<int-twitter:dm-outbound-channel-adapter
  twitter-template="twitterTemplate"
  channel="twitterSendDirectMessage"/>
```

Any message that is put on the `twitterSendDirectMessage` channel is sent to the user directly. But where is the name of the user to whom the message will be sent? It is decided by a header in the message `TwitterHeaders.DM_TARGET_USER_ID`. This must be populated either programmatically, or by using enrichers or SpEL. For example, it can be programmatically added as follows:

```
Message message = MessageBuilder.withPayload("Chandan")
  .setHeader(TwitterHeaders.DM_TARGET_USER_ID,
  "test_id").build();
```

Alternatively, it can be populated by using a header enricher, as follows:

```
<int:header-enricher input-channel="twitterIn"
  output-channel="twitterOut">
  <int:header name="twitter_dmTargetUserId" value=" test_id "/>
</int:header-enricher>
```

Twitter search outbound gateway

As gateways provide a two-way window, the search outbound gateway can be used to issue dynamic search commands and receive the results as a collection. If no result is found, the collection is empty. Let's configure a search outbound gateway, as follows:

```
<int-twitter:search-outbound-gateway id="twitterSearch"
  request-channel="searchQueryChannel"
  twitter-template="twitterTemplate"
  search-args-expression="#springintegration"
  reply-channel="searchQueryResultChannel"/>
```

And here is what the tags covered in this code mean:

- `int-twitter:search-outbound-gateway`: This is the namespace for the Twitter search outbound gateway

- `request-channel`: This is the channel that is used to send search requests to this gateway

- `twitter-template`: This is the Twitter template reference

- `search-args-expression`: This is used as arguments for the search
- `reply-channel`: This is the channel on which searched results are populated

This gives us enough to get started with the social integration aspects of the spring framework.

Enterprise messaging

Enterprise landscape is incomplete without JMS—it is one of the most commonly used mediums of enterprise integration. Spring provides very good support for this. Spring Integration builds over that support and provides adapter and gateways to receive and consume messages from many middleware brokers such as ActiveMQ, RabbitMQ, Rediss, and so on.

Spring Integration provides inbound and outbound adapters to send and receive messages along with gateways that can be used in a request/reply scenario. Let's walk through these implementations in a little more detail. A basic understanding of the JMS mechanism and its concepts is expected. It is not possible to cover even the introduction of JMS here. Let's start with the prerequisites.

Prerequisites

To use Spring Integration messaging components, namespaces, and relevant Maven the following dependency should be added:

- Namespace support can be added by using the following code snippet:

```
xmlns: int-jms=
  "http://www.springframework.org/schema/integration/jms"
  xsi:schemaLocation="http://www.springframework.org/
  schema/integration/jms http://www.springframework.org/
  schema/integration/jms/spring-integration-jms.xsd">
```

- Maven entry can be provided using the following code snippet:

```
<dependency>
  <groupId>org.springframework.integration</groupId>
  <artifactId>spring-integration-jms</artifactId>
  <version>${spring.integration.version}</version>
</dependency>
```

After adding these two dependencies, we are ready to use the components. But before we can use an adapter, we must configure an underlying message broker. Let's configure ActiveMQ. Add the following in `pom.xml`:

```xml
<dependency>
  <groupId>org.apache.activemq</groupId>
  <artifactId>activemq-core</artifactId>
  <version>${activemq.version}</version>
  <exclusions>
    <exclusion>
      <artifactId>spring-context</artifactId>
      <groupId>org.springframework</groupId>
    </exclusion>
  </exclusions>
</dependency>
<dependency>
  <groupId>org.springframework</groupId>
  <artifactId>spring-jms</artifactId>
  <version>${spring.version}</version>
  <scope>compile</scope>
</dependency>
```

After this, we are ready to create a connection factory and JMS queue that will be used by the adapters to communicate. First, create a session factory. As you will notice, this is wrapped in Spring's `CachingConnectionFactory`, but the underlying provider is ActiveMQ:

```xml
<bean id="connectionFactory" class="org.springframework.
  jms.connection.CachingConnectionFactory">
  <property name="targetConnectionFactory">
    <bean class="org.apache.activemq.ActiveMQConnectionFactory">
      <property name="brokerURL" value="vm://localhost"/>
    </bean>
  </property>
</bean>
```

Let's create a queue that can be used to retrieve and put messages:

```xml
<bean
  id="feedInputQueue"
  class="org.apache.activemq.command.ActiveMQQueue">
  <constructor-arg value="queue.input"/>
</bean>
```

Now, we are ready to send and retrieve messages from the queue. Let's look into each message one by one.

Receiving messages – the inbound adapter

Spring Integration provides two ways of receiving messages: polling and event listener. Both of them are based on the underlying Spring framework's comprehensive support for JMS. `JmsTemplate` is used by the polling adapter, while `MessageListener` is used by the event-driven adapter. As the name suggests, a polling adapter keeps polling the queue for the arrival of new messages and puts the message on the configured channel if it finds one. On the other hand, in the case of the event-driven adapter, it's the responsibility of the server to notify the configured adapter.

The polling adapter

Let's start with a code sample:

```
<int-jms:inbound-channel-adapter
    connection-factory="connectionFactory"
    destination="feedInputQueue"
    channel="jmsProcessedChannel">
    <int:poller fixed-rate="1000" />
</int-jms:inbound-channel-adapter>
```

This code snippet contains the following components:

- `int-jms:inbound-channel-adapter`: This is the namespace support for the JMS inbound adapter
- `connection-factory`: This is the encapsulation for the underlying JMS provider setup, such as ActiveMQ
- `destination`: This is the JMS queue where the adapter is listening for incoming messages
- `channel`: This is the channel on which incoming messages should be put

There is a poller element, so it's obvious that it is a polling-based adapter. It can be configured in one of two ways: by providing a JMS template or using a connection factory along with a destination. I have used the latter approach. The preceding adapter has a polling queue mentioned in the destination and once it gets any message, it puts the message on the channel configured in the `channel` attribute.

The event-driven adapter

Similar to polling adapters, event-driven adapters also need a reference either to an implementation of the interface AbstractMessageListenerContainer or need a connection factory and destination. Again, I will use the latter approach. Here is a sample configuration:

```
<int-jms:message-driven-channel-adapter
    connection-factory="connectionFactory"
    destination="feedInputQueue"
    channel="jmsProcessedChannel"/>
```

There is no poller sub-element here. As soon as a message arrives at its destination, the adapter is invoked, which puts it on the configured channel.

Sending messages – the outbound adapter

Outbound adapters convert messages on the channel to JMS messages and put them on the configured queue. To convert Spring Integration messages to JMS messages, the outbound adapter uses JmsSendingMessageHandler. This is is an implementation of MessageHandler. Outbound adapters should be configured with either JmsTemplate or with a connection factory and destination queue. Keeping in sync with the preceding examples, we will take the latter approach, as follows:

```
<int-jms:outbound-channel-adapter
    connection-factory="connectionFactory"
    channel="jmsChannel"
    destination="feedInputQueue"/>
```

This adapter receives the Spring Integration message from jmsChannel, converts it to a JMS message, and puts it on the destination.

Gateway

Gateway provides a request/reply behavior instead of a one-way send or receive. For example, after sending a message, we might expect a reply or we may want to send an acknowledgement after receiving a message.

The inbound gateway

Inbound gateways provide an alternative to inbound adapters when request-reply capabilities are expected. An inbound gateway is an event-based implementation that listens for a message on the queue, converts it to Spring `Message`, and puts it on the channel. Here is a sample code:

```
<int-jms:inbound-gateway
   request-destination="feedInputQueue"
   request-channel="jmsProcessedChannel"/>
```

However, this is what an inbound adapter does—even the configuration is similar, except the namespace. So, what is the difference? The difference lies in replying back to the reply destination. Once the message is put on the channel, it will be propagated down the line and at some stage a reply would be generated and sent back as an acknowledgement. The inbound gateway, on receiving this reply, will create a JMS message and put it back on the reply destination queue. Then, where is the reply destination? The reply destination is decided in one of the following ways:

1. Original message has a property `JMSReplyTo`, if it's present it has the highest precedence.

2. The inbound gateway looks for a configured, default-reply-destination which can be configured either as a name or as a direct reference of a channel. For specifying channel as direct reference default-reply-destination tag should be used.

An exception will be thrown by the gateway if it does not find either of the preceding two ways.

The outbound gateway

Outbound gateways should be used in scenarios where a reply is expected for the send messages. Let's start with an example:

```
<int-jms:outbound-gateway
   request-channel="jmsChannel"
   request-destination="feedInputQueue"
   reply-channel="jmsProcessedChannel" />
```

The preceding configuration will send messages to `request-destination`. When an acknowledgement is received, it can be fetched from the configured `reply-destination`. If `reply-destination` has not been configured, JMS `TemporaryQueues` will be created.

HTTP

Spring Integration provides support to access external HTTP services as well as to expose HTTP services to an external application.

Prerequisites

Let's add a namespace and relevant Maven dependency so that Spring Integration's HTTP components are available for use in our application:

- Namepace support can be added using the following code snippet:

```
<beans xmlns=
  "http://www.springframework.org/schema/beans"
  xmlns:xsi=
  "http://www.w3.org/2001/XMLSchema-instance"
  xmlns:int=
  "http://www.springframework.org/schema/integration"
  xmlns:int-http=
  "http://www.springframework.org/schema/integration/http"
  xsi:schemaLocation=
  "http://www.springframework.org/schema/beans http://www.
  springframework.org/schema/beans/spring-beans.xsd
  http://www.springframework.org/schema/integration http://www.
  springframework.org/schema/integration/spring-integration.xsd
  http://www.springframework.org/schema/integration/http
  http://www.springframework.org/schema/integration/http/spring-
  integration-http.xsd">
```

- Maven entry can be added using the following code:

```
<dependency>
  <groupId>org.springframework.integration</groupId>
  <artifactId>spring-integration-http</artifactId>
  <version>${spring.integration.version}</version>
</dependency>
<dependency>
  <groupId>org.springframework</groupId>
  <artifactId>spring-webmvc</artifactId>
  <version>${spring.version}</version>
</dependency>
```

The HTTP inbound gateway

Inbound gateways expose HTTP services to the external world, for example, REST-based web services. The application must be deployed in a web container such as Jetty or Tomcat for the inbound adapter or the gateway to work. The easiest way to implement the inbound component is by using Spring's `HttpRequestHandlerServlet` class, and by defining it in the `web.xml` file. Here is a sample entry:

```
<servlet>
  <servlet-name>inboundGateway</servlet-name>
  <servlet-class> o.s.web.context.support.
    HttpRequestHandlerServlet
  </servlet-class>
</servlet>
```

Alternatively, we can use the spring MVC support. This is what we have used in our example; let's take a look at the `web.xml` file:

```
<?xml version="1.0" encoding="UTF-8"?>
<web-app xmlns:xsi="http://www.w3.org/2001/XMLSchema-instance"
  xmlns="http://java.sun.com/xml/ns/javaee" xmlns:web="http://java.
  sun.com/xml/ns/javaee/web-app_2_5.xsd" xsi:schemaLocation="http://
  java.sun.com/xml/ns/javaee http://java.sun.com/xml/ns/javaee/web-
  app_2_5.xsd" id="WebApp_ID" version="2.5">
  <display-name>testhttpinbound</display-name>
  <servlet>
    <servlet-name>testhttpinbound</servlet-name>
    <servlet-class>org.springframework.web.
      servlet.DispatcherServlet</servlet-class>
    <init-param>
      <param-name>contextConfigLocation</param-name>
      <param-value>/WEB-INF/http-inbound-config.xml</param-value>
    </init-param>
    <load-on-startup>1</load-on-startup>
  </servlet>
  <servlet-mapping>
    <servlet-name>testhttpinbound</servlet-name>
    <url-pattern>/*</url-pattern>
  </servlet-mapping>
</web-app>
```

The `org.springframework.web.servlet.DispatcherServlet` class is a standard Spring MVC controller. Notice the configuration parameter, `http-inbound-config.xml`. This is the file that will have the declaration for the gateway:

```
<int-http:inbound-gateway
  request-channel="receiveChannel"
  path="receiveGateway"
  supported-methods="GET"/>
```

The components used in this code are explained in the following bullet points:

- `int-http:inbound-gateway`: This is the namespace support for the HTML gateway
- `request-channel`: This will put the incoming request payload on the channel
- `path`: This is the path exposed for incoming requests
- `supported-methods`: This is a comma-separated list of supported methods that use the HTTP protocol

In the following code, the service activator listens for the payload on the input channel and modifies it before an inbound gateway sends a response:

```
<int:service-activator
   input-channel="receiveChannel"
   expression="payload + ' hmm, you get what you give!!'"/>
```

`HttpMessageConverter` can be used to convert `HttpServletRequest` to `Messages`. A gateway element produces different instances depending on whether it has to return just a response (for example 200 success) or it has to return a response with a view. If the response is a view, it produces an instance of `HttpRequestHandlingController`. Otherwise, it produces an instance of `HandlingMessagingGateway`. To render the view, any view-rendering technology supported by Spring MVC can be used.

For requests that just require a confirmation that the request was successful, an adapter can be used instead of the gateway:

```
<int-http:inbound-channel-adapter
   channel="testchannel"
   supported-methods="GET,POST"
   name="/test"
   view-name="testMessageView" />
```

The HTTP outbound gateway

The outbound gateway is used to invoke services published by external HTTP components. Let's use our preceding example to test this. Create a war of the application that has inbound gateways and deploy it in a container. We can use the following example of an outbound gateway to invoke the HTTP request:

```
<int-http:outbound-gateway
   request-channel="outboundRequestChannel"
   url="http://localhost:8080/httpinbound/receiveGateway"
   http-method="GET"
   expected-response-type="java.lang.String"/>
```

The components used in this code are explained in the following bullet points:

- `int-http:outbound-gateway`: This is the namespace support for the HTTP outbound gateway
- `channel`: Based on the message on this channel, it will try to hit the URL
- `url`: This is the external URL to which a request is made
- `http-method`: This specifies which HTTP methods should be used while making the request
- `expected-response-type`: This is the type of response expected (by default, it's `String`)

Instead of gateway, adapters can also be used. The only difference is that an adapter does not send a response back on the reply channel. Under the hood, outbound adapters use the `RestTemplate` from the Spring framework. The following code snippet adds the outbound adapter:

```
<int-http:outbound-channel-adapter
  id="feedAdapter"
  url=" http://localhost:8080/httpinbound/receiveGateway"
  channel="feedUpdates"
  http-method="POST"/>
```

Web services

The HTTP adapter and gateways provide support for REST-based web services, but Spring Integration also provides support for XML-based web services such as SOAP. An inbound adapter or gateway is used to create and expose an endpoint as a web service, while an outbound adapter or gateway is used to invoke external services. Spring Integration support for web services is built over the spring `ws` project. I am not going to cover spring `ws` or any specific SOAP details such as `wsdl`, header, body, or payload. Instead, we will showcase the Spring Integration wrappers.

Prerequisites

Web services support can be added by including the following namespaces and Maven dependencies:

- Namespace support can be added using the following code snippet:
  ```
  <beans xmlns=
    "http://www.springframework.org/schema/beans"
    xmlns:xsi=
    "http://www.w3.org/2001/XMLSchema-instance"
  ```

```
xmlns:int=
"http://www.springframework.org/schema/integration"
xmlns:int-ws=
"http://www.springframework.org/schema/integration/ws"
xsi:schemaLocation=
"http://www.springframework.org/schema/integration/ws http://
www.springframework.org/schema/integration/ws/spring-
integration-ws.xsd
http://www.springframework.org/schema/integration http://www.
springframework.org/schema/integration/spring-integration.xsd
http://www.springframework.org/schema/beans http://www.
springframework.org/schema/beans/spring-beans.xsd">
```

- Maven entry can be added using the following code:

```
<dependency>
    <groupId>org.springframework.integration</groupId>
    <artifactId>spring-integration-xml</artifactId>
    <version>${spring.integration.version}</version>
</dependency>
<dependency>
    <groupId>org.springframework.integration</groupId>
    <artifactId>spring-integration-ws</artifactId>
    <version>${spring.integration.version}</version>
</dependency>
<dependency>
    <groupId>com.sun.xml.messaging.saaj</groupId>
    <artifactId>saaj-impl</artifactId>
    <version>${saaj.version}</version>
</dependency>
<dependency>
    <groupId>javax.activation</groupId>
    <artifactId>activation</artifactId>
    <version>${javax-activation.version}</version>
</dependency>
```

The inbound gateway

Inbound gateways will expose a SOAP service for handling an external request, which will then be converted to messages and posted to the channel. A front controller is required to intercept requests and pass them on the configured gateway; it is an instance of `org.springframework.ws.transport.http.MessageDispatcherServlet`. This should be configured in the `web.xml` file:

```
<?xml version="1.0" encoding="ISO-8859-1" standalone="no"?>
<web-app xmlns="http://java.sun.com/xml/ns/j2ee" xmlns:xsi="http://
    www.w3.org/2001/XMLSchema-instance" version="2.4"
    xsi:schemaLocation="http://java.sun.com/xml/ns/j2ee http://java.sun.
    com/xml/ns/j2ee/web-app_2_4.xsd">
```

```
    <description>ws-inbound-webservice</description>

<servlet>
  <servlet-name>springwsinbound</servlet-name>
  <servlet-class>
    org.springframework.ws.transport.http.MessageDispatcherServlet
  </servlet-class>
  <init-param>
    <param-name>contextConfigLocation</param-name>
    <param-value>
      WEB-INF/ws-inbound-config.xml
    </param-value>
  </init-param>
  <load-on-startup>1</load-on-startup>
</servlet>

  <servlet-mapping>
    <servlet-name>springwsinbound</servlet-name>
    <url-pattern>/testwsservice</url-pattern>
  </servlet-mapping>

  <welcome-file-list>
    <welcome-file>index.html</welcome-file>
  </welcome-file-list>

</web-app>
```

An implementation of `org.springframework.ws.server.EndpointMapping` must be provided to do the mapping between servlet and an endpoint. This can be configured either in the Java configuration class or property file. Let's put it in a property file and inject it as `contextConfigLocation`:

```
<bean class=
  "org.springframework.ws.server.endpoint.mapping.UriEndpointMapping">
  <property name="defaultEndpoint" ref="ws-inbound-gateway"/>
</bean>
```

The `org.springframework.ws.server.endpoint.mapping.UriEndpointMapping` class performs servlet to `Message` mapping.

After that, we have the service activator that can change the response or do some operations on it:

```
<int:channel id="input"/>

<int-ws:inbound-gateway
  id="ws-inbound-gateway"
```

```
request-channel="input"/>

  <int:service-activator
    input-channel="input">
    <bean class="com.cpandey.siexample.TestWsInbound"/>
  </int:service-activator>
```

The outbound gateway

This is even easier; the outbound gateway can take a URI and invoke the service, as follows:

```
<int-ws:outbound-gateway
  uri=" http://www.w3schools.com/webservices/tempconvert.asmx"
  request-channel=" fahrenheitChannel"
  reply-channel="responses" />
```

In the preceding code, a valid SOAP payload should be put on the `request-channel`; this will be used by the gateway to invoke the service configured. The payload of the response is published on the `reply-channel`. Here is an example code snippet to invoke the preceding service:

```
ClassPathXmlApplicationContext context =
  new ClassPathXmlApplicationContext
  ("/META-INF/spring/integration/temperatureConversion.xml");

DestinationResolver<MessageChannel> channelResolver = new
  BeanFactoryChannelResolver(context);

// Compose the XML message according to the server's schema

String requestXml =
  "<FahrenheitToCelsius
  xmlns=\"http://www.w3schools.com/webservices/\">" +
  "    <Fahrenheit>90.0</Fahrenheit>" +
  "</FahrenheitToCelsius>";

// Create the Message object
Message<String> message = MessageBuilder.withPayload
  (requestXml).build();

// Send the Message to the handler's input channel
MessageChannel channel = channelResolver.resolveDestination("fahrenhe
  itChannel");
channel.send(message);
```

Database SQL

It's difficult to imagine enterprise applications without any database; it is one of the oldest and most commonly used bridging mechanisms. Spring Integration provides support to read from and write to the database. Again, this support is based on the Spring framework's foundation for database support. It provides inbound and outbound adapters, gateways, and even specific adapters for stored procedures. Let's have a look at some of these, and others can be used on the same pattern.

Prerequisites

Before we talk about how to use database support of Spring Integration, let's add the necessary namespaces and Maven dependencies:

- Namespace support can be added using the following code snippet:

```
xmlns:int-jdbc=
"http://www.springframework.org/schema/integration/jdbc"
xmlns:jdbc=
"http://www.springframework.org/schema/jdbc"
xsi:schemaLocation="
http://www.springframework.org/schema/integration/jdbc
http://www.springframework.org/schema/integration/jdbc/spring-
integration-jdbc.xsd
http://www.springframework.org/schema/jdbc http://www.
springframework.org/schema/jdbc/spring-jdbc.xsd>
```

- Maven entry can be added using the following code snippet:

```
<dependency>
  <groupId>org.springframework.integration</groupId>
  <artifactId>spring-integration-jdbc</artifactId>
  <version>${spring.integration.version}</version>
</dependency>
```

Datasource

Before we can start using the component, we need to define a datasource. Datasource is a wrapper that encapsulates database connection details. A sample datasource for an in-memory database H2 is as follows:

```
<jdbc:embedded-database id="dataSource" type="H2"/>
```

For simplicity, I will use an in-memory database. But this is nothing specific to Spring Integration; datasource can be configured for any database supported by Spring. Include the following dependency in `pom.xml` for the in-memory database:

```
<dependency>
  <groupId>com.h2database</groupId>
  <artifactId>h2</artifactId>
  <version>1.3.168</version>
</dependency>
```

Now, we are ready with the datasource. Let's initialize it with some test data; again, Spring provides easy-to-use components that can get our task done in a couple of lines of configuration:

```
<jdbc:initialize-database data-source="dataSource"
  ignore-failures="DROPS">
  <jdbc:script location="classpath:H2DB-DropScript.sql" />
  <jdbc:script location="classpath:H2DB-CreateScript.sql" />
  <jdbc:script location="classpath:H2DB-InsertScript.sql" />
</jdbc:initialize-database>
```

With the preceding configuration, we are now ready to explore the adapters, gateways, and other components provided by Spring.

Reading from the database – the inbound adapter

The inbound adapter needs a reference to `JdbcTemplate` or datasource. We will stick to datasource. Its task is to read data from the database and put the result on the specified channel. By default, the message payload is the whole result set expressed as a list. The result set type can be changed by defining the `RowMapper` strategy, support for which is provided by spring:

```
<int-jdbc:inbound-channel-adapter channel="printSqlResult"
  data-source="dataSource"
  query="select * from PEOPLE where name = 'Chandan'"
  update="update PEOPLE set name = 'ChandanNew'
  where name = 'Chandan'">
</int-jdbc:inbound-channel-adapter>
```

The contents of this code snippet have been explained in the following bullet points:

- `int-jdbc:inbound-channel-adapter`: This is the namespace support for the inbound channel adapter
- `data-source`: This is a reference to the datasource that encapsulates database connection details
- `query`: This is the query to be fired
- `update`: This is any update query to be fired that can be used to avoid duplicate processing

This configuration will connect to the database configured in the datasource. In our case, it's an in-memory database, that is, H2. It will execute the query and issue an update. The result will be put on the configured channel. The update query is very handy when we want to filter out already processed records in the next polling cycle.

Transaction support

Transaction support for the inbound adapter can be wrapped along with the poller:

```
<int-jdbc:inbound-channel-adapter
  query="somequery"
  channel="testChannel"
  data-source="dataSource" update="someupdate">
    <int:poller fixed-rate="1000">
      <int:transactional/>
    </int:poller>
</int-jdbc:inbound-channel-adapter>
```

With transaction as a sub-element of poller, query and update will be executed in the same transaction. A valid transaction manager should be defined; again it's nothing specific to Spring Integration. Instead, spring-based entity manager and transaction manager should be defined (again, this is nothing to do with Spring Integration; instead, it's standard spring database support stuff). The code is as follows:

```
<bean id="transactionManager"
  class=
  "org.springframework.orm.jpa.JpaTransactionManager">
  <constructor-arg ref="entityManagerFactory" />
</bean>

<bean id="entityManagerFactory"
  class=
  "org.springframework.orm.jpa.LocalContainerEntityManagerFactoryBean">
  <property name="dataSource"              ref="dataSource" />
```

```xml
    <property name="jpaVendorAdapter"    ref="vendorAdaptor"/>
    <property name="packagesToScan"    value="com.cpandey.siexample.
      pojo"/>
</bean>

<bean id="abstractVendorAdaptor" abstract="true">
  <property name="generateDdl" value="true" />
  <property name="database"    value="H2" />
  <property name="showSql"      value="false"/>
</bean>

<bean id="entityManager"
  class=
  "org.springframework.orm.jpa.support.SharedEntityManagerBean">
  <property name="entityManagerFactory" ref="entityManagerFactory"/>
</bean>

<bean id="vendorAdaptor"
  class=
  "org.springframework.orm.jpa.vendor.HibernateJpaVendorAdapter"
  parent="abstractVendorAdaptor">
</bean>
```

Writing to the database – the outbound adapter

The outbound adapter can be used to insert data in the database; it can use the message on the channel to construct the query and execute it. The following code will add the outbound adapter:

```xml
<int-jdbc:outbound-channel-adapter
  channel="printSqlResult"
  data-source="dataSource"
  query="insert into PEOPLE p(ID, NAME, CREATED_DATE_TIME) values(2,
  :payload[NAME], NOW())">
</int-jdbc:outbound-channel-adapter>
```

This extracts a value from the payload and writes the data in the database. The database to which data will be written depends on the datasource.

Inbound and outbound gateways

Gateways combine input and output adapter functionalities; it fires a query and posts the reply on the reply channel:

```
<int-jdbc:outbound-gateway
  update="insert into PEOPLE (ID, NAME, CREATED_DATE_TIME) values (3,
  :payload[NAME], NOW())"
  request-channel="insertChannel"
  reply-channel="printSqlResult"
  data-source="dataSource" />
```

Outbound gateways require a reference to the datasource that is used to decide the database to connect to.

Stream processing

Spring Integration provides two implicit components for stream: one to read the streams and an other to write to streams. This section is small—let's quickly get to the code!

Prerequisites

First, let's add the namespaces and Maven dependencies:

- Namespace support can be added using the following code:

```
<?xml version="1.0" encoding="UTF-8"?>
  <beans:beans xmlns:int-stream=
    "http://www.springframework.org/schema/
    integration/stream"
    xmlns:xsi="http://www.w3.org/2001/XMLSchema-instance"
    xmlns:beans="http://www.springframework.org/
    schema/beans"
    xsi:schemaLocation=
    "http://www.springframework.org/schema/beans
    http://www.springframework.org/schema/beans/
    spring-beans.xsd
    http://www.springframework.org/schema/integration/
    stream
    http://www.springframework.org/schema/integration/
    stream/spring-integration-stream.xsd">
```

- Maven dependencies can be added using the following code snippet:

```
<dependency>
    <groupId>org.springframework.integration</groupId>
    <artifactId>spring-integration-stream</artifactId>
    <version>${spring.integration.version}</version>
</dependency>
```

With the previous inclusion, we are ready to use the adapters.

Reading from a stream

There is a STDIN adapter provided by Spring Integration that reads from `stdin`.
What is this `stdin`? Any stuff that is written to the command line, for example,
`System.in` in Java. The following code snippet is used to add the STDIN adapter:

```
<int-stream:stdin-channel-adapter
    id="stdin"
    channel="stdInChannel"/>
```

Here, `int-stream:stdin-channel-adapter` is the namespace support and channel
where the adapter puts the messages that have been written to the console.

If we want to get some insider view, spring uses either
`ByteStreamReadingMessageSource` or `CharacterStreamReadingMessageSource`,
which are implementations of `MessageSource`, to provide the adapter
functionality. `ByteStreamReadingMessageSource` needs `InputStream`, while
`CharacterStreamReadingMessageSource` needs `Reader`, as shown in the following
code snippet:

```
<bean
    class=
    "org.springframework.integration.stream.
    ByteStreamReadingMessageSource">
    <constructor-arg ref="inputStream"/>
</bean>

<bean
    class="org.springframework.integration.stream.
    CharacterStreamReadingMessageSource">
    <constructor-arg ref="reader"/>
</bean>
```

Writing to a stream

A similar adapter for writing to the console is also provided by Spring: `stdout`. It prints to the console whatever message it gets on the channel. Let's plug a `stdout` adapter to the preceding code and the output will be directed to the console:

```
<int-stream:stdout-channel-adapter
  id="stdout"
  channel="stdInChannel"
  append-newline="true"/>
```

`int-stream:stdout-channel-adapter` is the namespace, and channel is what the adapter will be polling for messages, and then print each on the console. `append-newline` will add a new line to output.

Behind the scenes, Spring uses either `ByteStreamWritingMessageHandler` or `CharacterStreamWritingMessageHandler`. They require a reference of `OutputStream` and `Writer`, respectively:

```
<bean
  class="org.springframework.integration.stream.
  ByteStreamWritingMessageHandler">
  <constructor-arg ref="outputStream"/>
</bean>

<bean
  class="org.springframework.integration.stream.
  CharacterStreamWritingMessageHandler">
  <constructor-arg ref="writer"/>
</bean>
```

This has been a long chapter and we all deserve a coffee break!

Summary

This chapter showcased the simplicity and abstraction that Spring Integration provides when it comes to handling complicated integrations, be it file-based, HTTP, JMS, or any other integration mechanism. Do not panic; I promise that the next few chapters are going to be smaller, and we will cover the testability of Spring Integration, performance, management, and then wrap up with an end-to-end example. In the next chapter, we will cover how Spring Batch and Spring Integration can be integrated to leverage the best of each framework.

7
Integration with Spring Batch

Today, a common user deals with web applications, mobile applications, and desktop software. All of these are interactive, which means they take user input and respond in real time. They might not even be aware of other kinds of applications—applications that run in the background, do not need continuous user interaction, and may go on for hours, days, or even weeks! Yes, I am talking about the batch job that is typically used for offline processing such as file type conversions, reporting, data mining, and so on. In the early days, machines were too slow and someone had to sit for hours to get a simple job done. In batch processing, you submit jobs and then go and do other work—you only come to collect the result! This revolutionized the computing world and justified the exorbitantly high prices of equipment and programmers. It would not be an exaggeration to say that batch jobs showed the real power and usefulness of computers.

If batch jobs are so important, it's obvious that Spring would have a very good support for it. Spring Batch is the module that provides comprehensive support for batch processing. In this chapter, we will look into how Spring Integration integrates with the Spring Batch module. In sync with the Spring philosophy of modular approach, each module works independently and at the same time provides the necessary interfaces to be easily integrated with others in the family. Spring Integration can interact with the Spring Batch module via messaging and can provide an event-driven mechanism to trigger batch jobs. This chapter will cover two aspects:

- A brief introduction to Spring Batch
- Spring Integration and Spring Batch

Spring Batch

For a layman, a batch job can be defined as any job that can be run offline. Typically, it will be a manual trigger and the result can be collected after the expected completion time. If all goes well, then it's really cool, but let's list some of the challenges:

- What if the external system that is used for a batch job (say an FTP server that hosts files) fails?

- If the machine running a batch job is rebooted for some reason, will the batch job also restart?

- What if some explicit parameters are required (for example, authentication details that might not be eligible for automation)?

- Will incomplete tasks be tried again or left out?

- How do we deal with transaction and rollback?

- How do we trigger and schedule the job at fixed intervals or in an event-driven fashion?

- If the jobs run in a thread, who will manage resource synchronization?

- How do we deal with the failures? Can the batch job trigger some alarm or send out notifications?

There are a lot of things that need to be accounted for — just imagine the difficulty if each of them has to be implemented by the programmer! Do not worry; Spring Batch is there to help you. With the help of Spring Integration, even the initial triggering part can be programmed — manual interaction is not required at all.

First of all, Spring Batch is not a scheduling framework like Quartz, Tivoli, and others — rather, it leverages these frameworks. It is a very lightweight framework that provides reusable components to address most of the concerns raised previously, for example, transaction support, database support for recoverable jobs, logging, auditing, and so on. Let's start with the configuration step and then we can move up to the examples.

Prerequisites

Before we can use the Spring Batch module, we need to add namespace support and Maven dependencies:

- **Namespace support**: Namespace support can be added by using the following code:

```
<beans xmlns="http://www.springframework.org/schema/beans"
    xmlns:batch="http://www.springframework.org/schema/batch"
```

```
xmlns:xsi="http://www.w3.org/2001/XMLSchema-instance"
xmlns:context="http://www.springframework.org/schema/context"
xmlns:int="http://www.springframework.org/schema/integration"
xsi:schemaLocation="http://www.springframework.org/schema/bea
ns
http://www.springframework.org/schema/beans/spring-
beans.xsd
http://www.springframework.org/schema/batch
http://www.springframework.org/schema/batch/
  spring-batch.xsd
http://www.springframework.org/schema/context
http://www.springframework.org/schema/context/spring-
context.xsd
http://www.springframework.org/schema/integration
http://www.springframework.org/schema/integration/spring-
integration.xsd">
```

- **Maven entry**: Maven entry support can be added by using the following code:

```
<dependency>
  <groupId>org.springframework.batch</groupId>
  <artifactId>spring-batch-core</artifactId>
  <version>3.0.1.RELEASE</version>
</dependency>

<dependency>
  <groupId>postgresql</groupId>
  <artifactId>postgresql</artifactId>
  <version>9.0-801.jdbc4</version>
</dependency>

<dependency>
  <groupId>commons-dbcp</groupId>
  <artifactId>commons-dbcp</artifactId>
  <version>1.4</version>
</dependency>
```

Defining a Spring Batch job

The unit of work in a Spring Batch is a *job*, which encapsulates all other aspects needed to complete a batch operation. Before we get into the details of how to configure and use Spring Batch components, let's familiarize ourselves with the basic terms used in a Spring Batch job.

The Spring Batch job language

Let's familiarize ourselves with the basic domain language of Spring Batch, which will help us understand the example:

- `Job`: This represents a batch process, and it has one-to-one mapping. For each batch process, there will be one job. It can be defined either in XML or the Java configuration — I have used the XML approach.

- `Step`: This is the logical breakdown of a job — a job has one or more steps. It encapsulates the phases of a job. A step is the logical unit that contains the actual details for running and controlling the batch job. Each job step can specify its fault tolerance — for example, skip an item on error, halt the job, and so on.

- `JobInstance`: This is one instance of a job. For example, a job must be run once a day, and each day run will be represented by a `JobInstance`.

- `JobParameter`: This is the parameter that is necessary for a `JobInstance` to complete.

- `JobExcecution`: When a `JobInstance` of a job is triggered, it may complete or fail. Each trigger of `JobInstance` is wrapped as `JobExecution`. So, for example, if a retry has been set and `JobInstance` is triggered thrice (due to failures) before it completes, then there are three instances of `JobExecution`.

- `StepExecution`: Similar to `JobExecution`, `StepExecution` is an instance of a single attempt to run a step. If a step completes after n retries, there will be n instances of `StepExecution`.

- `ExecutionContext`: One of the important aspects of the batch job is the ability to restart and reschedule failed jobs; for that, it's necessary to store enough information so that it can be triggered back, similar to a process context at the operating systemlevel. `ExecutionContext` is used to address this use case, which provides storage of key/value pairs of context-related properties.

- `JobRepository`: This is the persistence wrapper for all the aforementioned units. The underlying database provider can be from one of the many supported by Spring Batch.

- `JobLauncher`: This is an interface that is used to launch a job.

- `ItemReader`: This is an interface used by the step to read input. If the input set has been exhausted, `ItemReader` should indicate this by returning null.

- `ItemWriter`: This is the output interface of a step — one batch or chunk of items at a time.

- ItemProcessor: This is the intermediate state of ItemReader and ItemWriter. It provides the opportunity to apply transformation or business logic to an item.

With the preceding introduction, we can understand the Spring Batch example a little bit better. So let's start with one and define a batch job:

```
<batch:job id="importEmployeeRecords"
  job-repository="jobRepository"
  parent="simpleJob">
  <batch:step id="loadEmployeeRecords">
    <batch:tasklet>
      <batch:chunk
        reader="itemReader"
        writer="itemWriter"
        commit-interval="5"/>
    </batch:tasklet>
  </batch:step>
  <!-- Listener for status of JOB -->
  <batch:listeners>
    <batch:listener
      ref="notificationExecutionsListener"/>
  </batch:listeners>
</batch:job>
```

Here is the brief description of the tags used in the preceding configuration:

- batch:job: This is the parent tag that starts the definition of the batch job. id is used to uniquely identify this job, for example, to refer inside a JobLauncher to launch this job.

- batch:step: This is one of the steps for this job.

- batch:tasklet: This is the implementation that does the actual task of the step, leaving the step to take care of status maintenance, eventing, and so on.

- batch:chunk: A tasklet can be a simple service or a very complex task, while a chunk is a logical unit of work that can be worked upon by a tasklet.

- batch:listeners: These are used to propagate the events. We will revisit this later in this chapter.

What are the reader and writer? As the name suggests, reader reads the chunk of data while writer writes them back. There are standard readers provided by Spring to read a CSV file, but we can provide our own implementation. Let's look at a reader and writer used for this example.

ItemReader

As mentioned in the previous section, a reader is used to read a chunk of data. The following code snippet uses the Spring framework's `FlatFileItemReader` reader to read data from a flat file:

```xml
<bean id="itemReader"
  class="org.springframework.batch.item.file.FlatFileItemReader"
  scope="step">
  <property name="resource"
    value="file:///#{jobParameters['input.file.name']}"/>
  <property name="lineMapper">
    <bean class=
      "org.springframework.batch.item.file.mapping.DefaultLineMapper">
      <property name="lineTokenizer">
        <bean class=
          "org.springframework.batch.item.file.transform.
          DelimitedLineTokenizer">
          <property name="names"
            value="name,designation,dept,address"/>
        </bean>
      </property>
      <property name="fieldSetMapper">
        <bean class=
          "com.cpandey.siexample.batch.EmployeeFieldSetMapper"/>
      </property>
    </bean>
  </property>
</bean>
```

The components used in the preceding code snippet are explained in the following bullet points:

- `itemReader`: This uses Spring's default flat file reader, whose location has been mentioned by the `resource` property. The name will be retrieved from the `JobParameter` item passed to the job. We will see how to pass it when we write the launcher.

- `lineMapper`: This is a default implementation from Spring that has been used to map a line from the CSV file.

- `lineTokenizer`: It is very important how each token on a line should be interpreted. The value of the property `names` decides the order. For example, in the preceding example, it is `name,designation,dept,address`, which means if a sample file has an entry like this:

```
Chandan, SWEngineer, RnD, India
Pandey, Tester, RnD, India
```

Then each chunk will be interpreted as name, designation, department, and address, respectively.

- `fieldSetMapper`: Although some default implementations are available, most of the time it is a custom class that defines the mapping between the item in a CSV file and the domain model. The following is the code snippet of our example that uses the mapper:

```
import org.springframework.batch.item.
  file.mapping.FieldSetMapper;
import org.springframework.batch.item.
  file.transform.FieldSet;
import org.springframework.validation.BindException;

public class EmployeeFieldSetMapper implements
  FieldSetMapper<Employee> {

@Override
public Employee mapFieldSet(FieldSet fieldSet)
  throws BindException {
    Employee employee = new Employee();
    employee.setName(fieldSet.readString("name"));
    employee.setDesignation
    (fieldSet.readString("designation"));
    employee.setDept(fieldSet.readString("dept"));
    employee.setAddress(fieldSet.readString("address"));
    return employee;
  }
}
```

ItemWriter

A writer is used to write chunks of data. A writer is almost always user defined. It can be defined to write in a file, database, or JMS, or to any endpoint—it depends on our implementation. Towards the end of the chapter, we will discuss how this can be used to even trigger an event in the Spring Integration environment. Let's first look at a simple writer configuration:

```
<bean id="itemWriter"
class="com.cpandey.siexample.batch.EmployeeRecordWriter"/>
```

The following code snippet is the implementation of the writer class:

```
import java.util.List;
import org.springframework.batch.item.ItemWriter;
public class EmployeeRecordWriter implements ItemWriter<Employee> {
```

```java
@Override
public void write(List<? extends Employee> employees) throws
Exception {
  if(employees!=null){
    for (Employee employee : employees) {
      System.out.println(employee.toString());
    }
  }
}
}
```

For simplicity, I have printed the records, but as mentioned previously, it can be populated in the database or it can be used to do whatever we want to do inside this class.

Okay, so far we have defined the job, the reader, and the writer; then what's stopping us from launching it? How do we launch this batch job? Spring provides the `Joblauncher` interface that can be used to launch the job. `Joblauncher` needs an interface of the type `JobRepository` to store the context of the job so that it can be recovered and restarted on failure. `JobRepository` can be configured to leverage any database that Spring can use, for example, in-memory, MySql, PostGres, and so on. Let's define `jobLauncher` as follows:

```xml
<bean id="jobLauncher"
  class="org.springframework.batch.core.launch.
  support.SimpleJobLauncher">
  <property name="jobRepository" ref="jobRepository"/>
</bean>
```

Since `JobLauncher` cannot be used without a `JobRepository`, let's configure JobRepository:

```xml
<bean id="jobRepository"
  class="org.springframework.batch.core.repository.support.
  MapJobRepositoryFactoryBean">
  <property name="transactionManager" ref="transactionManager"/>
</bean>
```

The moment we talk about persistence store, a data-source definition is needed that can abstract the database properties such as username, password, and so on. The following code snippet contains the configuration of a data source (this is an Apache DBCP implementation):

```java
import org.apache.commons.dbcp.BasicDataSource;
import org.springframework.beans.factory.annotation.Value;
import org.springframework.context.annotation.Bean;
```

```
import org.springframework.context.annotation.Configuration;
@Configuration
public class BatchJdbcConfiguration {
  @Value("${db.driverClassName}")
  private String driverClassName;
  @Value("${db.url}")
  private String url;
  @Value("${db.username}")
  private String username;
  @Value("${db.password}")
  private String password;
  @Bean(destroyMethod = "close")

  public BasicDataSource dataSource() {
    BasicDataSource dataSource = new BasicDataSource();
    dataSource.setDriverClassName(driverClassName);
    dataSource.setUrl(url);
    dataSource.setUsername(username);
    dataSource.setPassword(password);
    return dataSource;
  }
}
```

The properties shown in the preceding code can be configured in a properties file, let's say batch.properties. We can provide the properties in a class path and use the property-placeholder tag to inject the properties, as shown here:

```
<context:property-placeholder
  location="/META-INF/spring/integration/batch.properties"/>
  db.password=root
  db.username=postgres
  db.databaseName=postgres
  db.driverClassName=org.postgresql.Driver
  db.serverName=localhost:5432
  db.url=jdbc:postgresql://${db.serverName}/${db.databaseName}
```

As soon as the database is there, we need transactions! Let's configure the transaction manager:

```
<bean id="transactionManager"
  class="org.springframework.batch.support.transaction.
  ResourcelessTransactionManager" />
```

Thank god, no more configurations! By the way, these are not specific to any batch job; any data source and transaction manager configured in the existing application can be used. With all these configurations, we are ready to launch the batch job. Let's see the following sample code:

```java
import org.springframework.batch.core.Job;
import org.springframework.batch.core.JobExecution;
import org.springframework.batch.core.JobParametersBuilder;
import org.springframework.batch.core.
  JobParametersInvalidException;
import org.springframework.batch.core.launch.JobLauncher;
import org.springframework.batch.core.repository.
  JobExecutionAlreadyRunningException;
import org.springframework.batch.core.repository.
  JobInstanceAlreadyCompleteException;
import org.springframework.batch.core.repository.
  JobRestartException;
import org.springframework.context.ApplicationContext;
import org.springframework.context.support.
  ClassPathXmlApplicationContext;

public class BatchJobLauncher {
  public static void main(String[] args) throws
    JobExecutionAlreadyRunningException, JobRestartException,
    JobInstanceAlreadyCompleteException,
    JobParametersInvalidException {
    ApplicationContext context = new
      ClassPathXmlApplicationContext("/META-
      INF/spring/integration/spring-integration-batch.xml");
    Job job = context.getBean("importEmployeeRecords", Job.class);
    JobLauncher jobLauncher= context.getBean("jobLauncher",
      JobLauncher.class);
    JobParametersBuilder jobParametersBuilder = new
      JobParametersBuilder();
    jobParametersBuilder.addString("input.file.name",
      "C:/workspace_sts/siexample/src/main/resources/
      META-INF/spring/integration/employee.input");
    JobExecution execution =jobLauncher.
      run(job, jobParametersBuilder.toJobParameters());
  }
}
```

Let's understand the code:

- **Load the file**: We first load the configuration file.

- **Extract the reference**: The next step is to retrieve the reference of the defined job using its unique ID.

- **Add parameters**: A job needs a parameter, so we define `JobParameter` using the `JobParameterBuilder` class. The name of the file being passed as a value of the key is `input.file.name`, which was configured in the job definition.

- **Launch the job**: Finally, use Spring's `JobLauncher` class to launch the job.

Hmm! Now we have a small and simple batch up and running. Let's see how Spring Integration can be used to reap its power and enhance the usage even further.

Spring Batch and Spring Integration

Typically, a batch application can be triggered via a command-line interface or programmatically, for example, from a web container. Let's introduce Spring Integration and see the possibilities:

- It can be triggered on an event, for example, a file adapter listening for a file triggers Spring Integration on arrival of the file.

- Execution can be chained in a flow — trigger the job, pass on the result, invoke the error path, and so on.

- The message queue is not meant for huge amounts of data. So for big files, Spring Integration can act as the trigger, while delegating the actual task to Spring Batch. It can provide a strategy to chunk the files and distribute them across the Spring Batch job.

- Spring Integration not only triggers batch jobs, but can also collect the result and propagate it in the system. For example, a batch process triggered by Spring Integration may finish off in a day, after which `ItemWriter` can write an item to JMS on which the Spring Integration adapter is listening. Even without any awareness or locking in for the job started, messages from the queue will be processed by Spring Integration.

Launching the job

Enough theory! Let's write some code. This time, we will trigger the batch job on some event instead of triggering manually. We are processing a file, what if we process a file adapter? Let's write a file adapter that will listen for files in a directory and trigger a batch job on the availability of a file:

```
<int-file:inbound-channel-adapter id="fileAdapter"
  directory="C:\Chandan\Projects\inputfolderforsi"
  channel="filesOutputChannel"
  prevent-duplicates="true" filename-pattern="*.txt">
  <int:poller fixed-rate="1000" />
</int-file:inbound-channel-adapter>
```

No need to define the file adapter tags, as they have been taken care of in the previous chapter.

The preceding configuration will listen for files in the configured directory. Files will be put on to `fileOutPutChannel` as `Message<File>`, and we need to convert it to a form so that `JobLauncher` can understand it. We will use the `transformer` component:

```
<int:transformer
   input-channel="filesOutputChannel"
   output-channel="batchRequest">
   <bean class="com.cpandey.siexample.batch.
     FileMessageToJobRequest">
     <property name="job" ref="importEmployeeRecords"/>
     <property name="fileParameterName" value="input.file.name"/>
   </bean>
</int:transformer>
```

We will have to write the logic to convert `Message<File>` to `JobLaunchRequest`. The following code is a very simple transformer that extracts the file path from the payload of `Message` (which is `File`) and then adds the retrieved path as `JobParameter`. This job parameter is then used to launch the job using Spring's `JobLauncher`, as shown in the following code snippet:

```
import java.io.File;

import org.springframework.batch.core.Job;
import org.springframework.batch.core.JobParametersBuilder;
import org.springframework.batch.
   integration.launch.JobLaunchRequest;
import org.springframework.integration.annotation.Transformer;
import org.springframework.messaging.Message;

public class FileMessageToJobRequest {
   private Job job;
   private String fileParameterName;

   public void setFileParameterName(String fileParameterName) {
     this.fileParameterName = fileParameterName;
   }

   public void setJob(Job job) {
     this.job = job;
   }
```

```
@Transformer
public JobLaunchRequest toRequest(Message<File> message) {
JobParametersBuilder jobParametersBuilder = new
  JobParametersBuilder();

jobParametersBuilder.addString(fileParameterName,
  message.getPayload().getAbsolutePath());
return new JobLaunchRequest
  (job,jobParametersBuilder.toJobParameters());
}
}
```

With this code in place, whenever a new file arrives in the directory, a batch job is triggered using Spring Integration. Moreover, file adapter was just an example, any adapter or gateway—such as mail, JMS, FTP, and others—can be plugged in to trigger the batch processing.

Tracking the status of a batch job

Most of the time, we would want to have feedback about the task in progress—how can we do that? Spring Integration is an event-based framework so no surprise that we can configure listeners with a batch job. If you refer to the batch job definition at the beginning, it has a listener defined:

```
<batch:listeners>
  <batch:listener ref="simpleListener"/>
</batch:listeners>
```

This code can have a Spring Integration gateway as a listener, which listens for the notification and puts the status of the batch job (of the type JobExecution) on the defined channel:

```
<int:gateway id=" simpleListener"
  service-interface="org.springframework.batch.core.
  JobExecutionListener" default-request-channel=
  "jobExecutionsStatus"/>
```

The status will be available on a channel where we have our processing done. Let's plug in a simple service activator to print the status:

```
<int:service-activator
  ref="batchStatusServiceActivator"
  method="printStatus"
  input-channel="jobExecutionsStatus"/>

import org.springframework.batch.core.JobExecution;
```

```
import org.springframework.integration.annotation.MessageEndpoint;
import org.springframework.messaging.Message;

@MessageEndpoint
public class BatchStatusServiceActivator {
  public void printStatus(Message<JobExecution> status ) {
    if(status!=null){
      System.out.println("Status ::
        "+status.getPayload().toString());
    }
  }
}
```

The other way round

Spring Integration can launch the batch job, and Spring Batch can interact with the Spring Integration and trigger components. How can we do this? Spring Integration's event-based components can be a good option. Let's take a simple example:

- There is an inbound JMS adapter in the Spring Integration application that listens for messages on the queue and, based on that, triggers some action.

- How can we invoke this adapter from Spring Batch? We can define a custom `ItemWriter` class in Spring Batch that writes its output to the JMS queue where the Spring Integration component is listening.

- As soon as `ItemWriter` writes to the JMS queue, the inbound adapter picks it up and passes it down the line for further processing.

The preceding use case is just one example; we can gel the eventing mechanism of both the frameworks and achieve the required inter-app communication.

Summary

This completes our discussion on how Spring Integration and Spring Batch can intercommunicate. We covered the basics of Spring Batch, how it can be leveraged by Spring Integration to delegate the processing of huge payloads, how status can be tracked, and then in turn how Spring Batch can trigger events and start processing in the Spring Integration application!

In the next chapter, we will discuss one of the most important aspects — testing. Keep up the energy!

8
Testing Support

Test Driven Development (TDD) has revolutionized the way software is developed and deployed, and why not, every customer wants working software—and the best way to prove that it's working is to test it! Spring Integration is no exception—so how can we test that each of the "units" are working in isolation?—in fact it's even more important to test the units so that any integration issues can be easily isolated. For example, an FTP inbound gateway is dependent on external factors such as user roles on the FTP server, performance of the FTP server, network latency, and so on. How can we validate that the consumer connected to an FTP inbound gateway can process files without actually connecting to an FTP server? We can send "mock" messages to the channel, which will be treated by the consumer as though it arrived from an FTP server! All we want to prove is that, given that files arrive on the channel, the listener will do its job.

In this chapter, I will cover aspects of Spring Integration testing—and mostly, it's going to be a "show me the code" chapter! Here is the broad outline of topics covered:

- Testing messages
- Testing headers
- Handling errors
- Testing filters
- Testing splitters

Prerequisite

So what is needed for testing? JUnit of course! What else? The Spring framework and Spring Integration itself provide many mocks and support classes, which help in testing the application. Let's add maven dependencies for these classes:

```
<dependency>
  <groupId>org.springframework.integration</groupId>
```

```
      <artifactId>spring-integration-test</artifactId>
      <version>${spring.integration.version}</version>
   </dependency>
   <dependency>
     <groupId>junit</groupId>
     <artifactId>junit</artifactId>
     <version>${junit.version}</version>
   </dependency>
   <dependency>
     <groupId>org.springframework</groupId>
     <artifactId>spring-test</artifactId>
     <version>${spring.version}</version>
     <scope>test</scope>
   </dependency>
```

Testing messages

Spring Integration provides a class that can help to build certain payloads such as the following example:

```
Message<String> message =
   MessageBuilder.withPayload("Test").build()
```

These messages can be put on the channel by grabbing the handle of an actual channel definition. This can be used for negative as well as positive testing. For example, if a service activator listening on the channel expects a message with the payload type File, then putting a message with a payload String should indicate an error. Let's write a quick test for our transformer, which accepts Message with the payload SyndEntry and converts it to SoFeed. The following code snippet is our transformer class:

```
import org.springframework.messaging.Message;

import com.cpandey.siexample.pojo.SoFeed;
import com.sun.syndication.feed.synd.SyndEntry;

public class SoFeedDbTransformer {

  public SoFeed transformFeed(Message<SyndEntry> message){
    SyndEntry entry = message.getPayload();
    SoFeed soFeed=new SoFeed();
    soFeed.setTitle(entry.getTitle());
    soFeed.setDescription(entry.getDescription().getValue());
    soFeed.setCategories(entry.getCategories());
    soFeed.setLink(entry.getLink());
```

```
        soFeed.setAuthor(entry.getAuthor());

        System.out.println("JDBC"+soFeed.getTitle());
        return soFeed;
    }
}
```

As mentioned, it gets a message having a payload of the type `SyndEntry`. Let's write a simple test case that will pass only if the conversion from `SyndEntry` to `SoFeed` is successful:

```
import static org.junit.Assert.assertNotNull;
import static org.junit.Assert.assertNull;
import static org.junit.Assert.assertThat;
import static org.springframework.integration.test.
  matcher.PayloadMatcher.hasPayload;

import java.util.ArrayList;
import java.util.List;

import org.junit.Test;
import org.junit.runner.RunWith;
import org.springframework.beans.factory.annotation.Autowired;
import org.springframework.integration.channel.QueueChannel;
import org.springframework.integration.support.MessageBuilder;
import org.springframework.messaging.Message;
import org.springframework.messaging.MessageChannel;
import org.springframework.test.context.ContextConfiguration;
import org.springframework.test.context.
  junit4.SpringJUnit4ClassRunner;

import com.cpandey.siexample.pojo.SoFeed;
import com.sun.syndication.feed.synd.SyndCategoryImpl;
import com.sun.syndication.feed.synd.SyndContent;
import com.sun.syndication.feed.synd.SyndContentImpl;
import com.sun.syndication.feed.synd.SyndEntry;
import com.sun.syndication.feed.synd.SyndEntryImpl;

@ContextConfiguration
@RunWith(SpringJUnit4ClassRunner.class)
public class TestSoDBFeedTransformer {
  @Autowired
  MessageChannel filteredFeedChannel;
```

```
  @Autowired
  QueueChannel transformedChannel;

  @Test
  public void messageIsConvertedToEntity() {
    //Define a dummy domain Object
    SyndEntry entry =new SyndEntryImpl();
    entry.setTitle("Test");
    SyndContent content=new SyndContentImpl();
    content.setValue("TestValue");
    entry.setDescription(content);
    List<SyndCategoryImpl> catList=new
      ArrayList<SyndCategoryImpl>();
    entry.setCategories(catList);
    entry.setLink("TestLink");
    entry.setAuthor("TestAuthor");

//Define expected result
    SoFeed expectedSoFeed=new SoFeed();
    expectedSoFeed.setTitle(entry.getTitle());
    expectedSoFeed.setDescription(entry.getDescription
      ().getValue());

    expectedSoFeed.setCategories(entry.getCategories()
      );
    expectedSoFeed.setLink(entry.getLink());
    expectedSoFeed.setAuthor(entry.getAuthor());

    Message<SyndEntry> message =
      MessageBuilder.withPayload(entry).build();
    filteredFeedChannel.send(message);
    Message<?> outMessage =
      transformedChannel.receive(0);
    SoFeedsoFeedReceived
      =(SoFeed)outMessage.getPayload();
    assertNotNull(outMessage);
    assertThat(outMessage,
      hasPayload(soFeedReceived));
    outMessage = transformedChannel.receive(0);
    assertNull("Only one message expected",
      outMessage);
  }
```

In this code, the `@ContextConfiguration` annotation is used to load the context information. By default, it will look for a file name such as `<classname>-context.xml` and Java configuration classes annotated with `@Configuration`. In our case, it is `TestSoDBFeedTransformer-context.xml`. This contains information required to run the test, such as channel, services definitions, and others:

```xml
<?xml version="1.0" encoding="UTF-8"?>
  <beans xmlns="http://www.springframework.org/schema/beans"
    xmlns:xsi="http://www.w3.org/2001/XMLSchema-instance"
    xmlns:int="http://www.springframework.org/schema/integration"
      xsi:schemaLocation="http://www.springframework.org/
        schema/integration http://www.springframework.org/
        schema/integration/spring-integration.xsd
    http://www.springframework.org/schema/beans
      http://www.springframework.org/
      schema/beans/spring-beans.xsd">

    <int:channel id="filteredFeedChannel"/>
    <int:channel id="transformedChannel">
      <int:queue/>
    </int:channel>

    <bean id="feedDbTransformerBean"
      class="com.cpandey.siexample.
      transformer.SoFeedDbTransformer" />
    <!-- Transformers -->
    <int:transformer id="dbFeedTransformer"
      ref="feedDbTransformerBean"
      input-channel="filteredFeedChannel"
      method="transformFeed"
      output-channel="transformedChannel"/>
  </beans>
```

The components covered in this code are explained in detail in the following points:

- `@RunWith(SpringJUnit4ClassRunner.class)`: This defines which engine to run the tests on — nothing specific to Spring Integration.

- `@Autowired  MessageChannel filteredFeedChannel`: This autowires the channel definition from the context file — no need to explicitly load it to use.

- `@Autowired  QueueChannel transformedChannel`: This is similar to the preceding point and this autowires other channels as well.

Spring configuration prepares all the required elements—now let's take a look at what the test class does:

1. It creates a dummy `SyndEntry`.
2. It creates an expected `SoFeed` based on that `SyndEntry`.
3. It builds a message with a payload of the type `SyndEntry`.
4. It grabs the handle of the channel on which the transformer is plugged and puts the payload on it.

    This is where the transformer is tested, and an actual instance of transformer (and not a mocked one) that is listening on the channel is invoked.

5. Transformer does the transformation and puts the result on the output channel.
6. The test class grabs the handle of the output channel and reads the message.

    The actual transformed message on the output channel must match the expected message constructed.

With the preceding steps, we are able to test an actual transformer, the logic written without worrying much about the channels, or other Spring Integration elements that are in any way external to the system.

Testing headers

As we tested the payload, it's fairly easy to test headers. Let's write a header enricher and then a test case to validate it:

```
<int:header-enricher
  input-channel="filteredFeedChannel"
  output-channel="transformedChannel">
  <int:header name="testHeaderKey1"
    value="testHeaderValue1"/>
  <int:header name="testHeaderKey2"
    value="testHeaderValue2"/>
</int:header-enricher>
```

Headers will be added to any message that is put on `filteredFeedChannel`. The following code snippet is the test to verify whether these headers are added or not:

```
import static org.junit.Assert.assertThat;
import static org.springframework.integration.
  test.matcher.HeaderMatcher.hasHeader;
```

```
import static org.springframework.integration.
   test.matcher.HeaderMatcher.hasHeaderKey;

import org.junit.Test;
import org.junit.runner.RunWith;
import org.springframework.beans.factory.annotation.Autowired;
import org.springframework.integration.channel.QueueChannel;
import org.springframework.integration.support.MessageBuilder;
import org.springframework.messaging.Message;
import org.springframework.messaging.MessageChannel;
import org.springframework.test.context.ContextConfiguration;
import org.springframework.test.context.
   junit4.SpringJUnit4ClassRunner;

@ContextConfiguration
// default context name is <ClassName>-context.xml
@RunWith(SpringJUnit4ClassRunner.class)
public class TestSoHeaderAddition {
  @Autowired
  MessageChannel filteredFeedChannel;

  @Autowired
  QueueChannel transformedChannel;

  @Test
  public void headerIsAddedToEntity() {
    Message<String> message =
      MessageBuilder.withPayload("testheader").build();
    filteredFeedChannel.send(message);
    Message<?> outMessage =
      transformedChannel.receive(0);
    assertThat(outMessage,
      hasHeaderKey("testHeaderKey1"));
    assertThat(outMessage, hasHeader("testHeaderKey1",
      "testHeaderValue1"));
  }
}
```

Here, we build up a test message and put it on a channel. A header enricher is plugged in to the input channel, which adds a header to the payload. We verified this by extracting the message from the output channel.

Handling errors

So far so good, how about handling error scenarios? How to test negative use cases and what to do with the failed test case? The following code snippet will help us in these matters:

```
@Test(expected = MessageTransformationException.class)
public void errorReportedWhenPayloadIsWrong() {
  Message<String> message =
    MessageBuilder.withPayload("this should fail").build();
  filteredFeedChannel.send(message);
}
```

The input channel expects a message with the payload type SyndEntry, but if a message with a String payload is sent—this must throw an exception. This is what has been tested. This can be further enhanced to monitor certain types of exception on channels with the ability to validate user-defined propagated messages.

Testing filters

We have defined a filter that filters out all messages except java feed. What is so special about filters that we want to discuss them separately? If you remember, filters always return a Boolean value, indicating whether to pass on the message or drop it, based on whether or not it satisfies the condition. For ease of reference, the following code snippet is the filter that we have defined:

```
import java.util.List;
import org.springframework.messaging.Message;
import com.sun.syndication.feed.synd.SyndCategoryImpl;
import com.sun.syndication.feed.synd.SyndEntry;

public class SoFeedFilter {
  public boolean filterFeed(Message<SyndEntry> message){
    SyndEntry entry = message.getPayload();
    List<SyndCategoryImpl>
      categories=entry.getCategories();
    if(categories!=null&&categories.size()>0){
      for (SyndCategoryImpl category: categories) {

        if(category.getName().equalsIgnoreCase("java")){
          return true;
        }

      }
```

```
      }
      return false;
   }
}
```

Let's create a test context class to test this. It's always better to have a separate context class to test, so that it does not mess up the actual environment.

Now, we write our test cases – the first one is to validate that all the messages with the type java are allowed to pass through:

```
@Test
public void javaMessagePassedThrough() {
   SyndEntry entry =new SyndEntryImpl();
   entry.setTitle("Test");
   SyndContent content=new SyndContentImpl();
   content.setValue("TestValue");
   entry.setDescription(content);
   List<SyndCategoryImpl> catList=new
      ArrayList<SyndCategoryImpl>();
   SyndCategoryImpl category=new SyndCategoryImpl();
   category.setName("java");
   catList.add(category);
   entry.setCategories(catList);
   entry.setLink("TestLink");
   entry.setAuthor("TestAuthor");

   Message<SyndEntry> message =
      MessageBuilder.withPayload(entry).build();
   fetchedFeedChannel.send(message);
   Message<?> outMessage = filteredFeedChannel.receive(0);
   assertNotNull("Expected an output message", outMessage);
   assertThat(outMessage, hasPayload(entry));
}
```

The next code snippet is used to test whether any other message except the category java is dropped:

```
@Test
public void nonJavaMessageDropped() {
   SyndEntry entry =new SyndEntryImpl();
   entry.setTitle("Test");
   SyndContent content=new SyndContentImpl();
   content.setValue("TestValue");
   entry.setDescription(content);
   List<SyndCategoryImpl> catList=new
```

```
          ArrayList<SyndCategoryImpl>();
      SyndCategoryImpl category=new SyndCategoryImpl();
      category.setName("nonjava");
      catList.add(category);
      entry.setCategories(catList);
      entry.setLink("TestLink");
      entry.setAuthor("TestAuthor");

      Message<SyndEntry> message =
        MessageBuilder.withPayload(entry).build();
      fetchedFeedChannel.send(message);
      Message<?> outMessage = filteredFeedChannel.receive(0);
      assertNull("Expected no output message", outMessage);
    }
```

Splitter test

Let's discuss the last test—which is for splitters. The splitter that we defined is as follows:

```
import org.springframework.messaging.Message;

import com.sun.syndication.feed.synd.SyndCategoryImpl;
import com.sun.syndication.feed.synd.SyndEntry;

public class SoFeedSplitter {
  public List<SyndCategoryImpl>
    splitAndPublish(Message<SyndEntry> message) {
    SyndEntry syndEntry=message.getPayload();
    List<SyndCategoryImpl> categories=
      syndEntry.getCategories();
    return categories;
  }
}
```

This is a very simple splitter, which splits the payload in a list of category implementations. Our test context file is given in the following code snippet:

```
<?xml version="1.0" encoding="UTF-8"?>
<beans xmlns="http://www.springframework.org/schema/beans"
  xmlns:xsi="http://www.w3.org/2001/XMLSchema-instance"
  xmlns:int="http://www.springframework.org/schema/integration"
  xsi:schemaLocation="http://www.springframework.org/
    schema/integration http://www.springframework.org/
    schema/integration/spring-integration.xsd
```

```
      http://www.springframework.org/schema/beans
      http://www.springframework.org/schema/beans/spring-beans.xsd">

  <int:channel id="filteredFeedChannel"/>
  <int:channel id="splitFeedOutputChannel">
    <int:queue/>
  </int:channel>
  <bean id="splitterSoFeedBean"
    class="com.cpandey.siexample.splitter.SoFeedSplitter"/>
  <!-- Splitter -->
  <int:splitter ref="splitterSoFeedBean"
    method="splitAndPublish" input-channel="filteredFeedChannel"
  output-channel="splitFeedOutputChannel" />
</beans>
```

The following code snippet represents our test class:

```
import static org.junit.Assert.assertNotNull;
import static org.junit.Assert.assertNull;
import static org.junit.Assert.assertThat;
import static org.springframework.integration.
  test.matcher.HeaderMatcher.hasHeader;
import static org.springframework.integration.
  test.matcher.HeaderMatcher.hasHeaderKey;
import static org.springframework.integration.
  test.matcher.PayloadMatcher.hasPayload;

import java.util.ArrayList;
import java.util.List;

import org.junit.Test;
import org.junit.runner.RunWith;
import org.springframework.beans.factory.annotation.Autowired;
import org.springframework.integration.channel.QueueChannel;
import org.springframework.integration.support.MessageBuilder;
import org.springframework.messaging.Message;
import org.springframework.messaging.MessageChannel;
import org.springframework.test.context.ContextConfiguration;
import org.springframework.test.
  context.junit4.SpringJUnit4ClassRunner;

import com.cpandey.siexample.pojo.SoFeed;
import com.sun.syndication.feed.synd.SyndCategoryImpl;
import com.sun.syndication.feed.synd.SyndContent;
import com.sun.syndication.feed.synd.SyndContentImpl;
import com.sun.syndication.feed.synd.SyndEntry;
```

```
import com.sun.syndication.feed.synd.SyndEntryImpl;

@ContextConfiguration   // default context name is <ClassName>-
context.xml
@RunWith(SpringJUnit4ClassRunner.class)
public class TestSplitter {
  //Autowire required channels
  @Autowired
  MessageChannel filteredFeedChannel;

  @Autowired
  QueueChannel splitFeedOutputChannel;


  @Test
  public void javaMessagePassedThrough() {
    //Create MOCK payload
    //Create a SyndEntry Object
    SyndEntry entry =new SyndEntryImpl();
    entry.setTitle("Test");
    //Create a SyndContent to be used with entry
    SyndContent content=new SyndContentImpl();
    content.setValue("TestValue");
    entry.setDescription(content);
    //Create List which is expected on Channel
    List<SyndCategoryImpl> catList=new
      ArrayList<SyndCategoryImpl>();
    //Create Categories
    SyndCategoryImpl category1=new SyndCategoryImpl();
    category1.setName("java");
    category1.setTaxonomyUri("");
    SyndCategoryImpl category2=new SyndCategoryImpl();
    category2.setName("java");
    category2.setTaxonomyUri("");
    //Add categories
    catList.add(category1);
    catList.add(category2);
    //Complete entry
    entry.setCategories(catList);
    entry.setLink("TestLink");
    entry.setAuthor("TestAuthor");

    //Use Spring Integration util method to build a payload
    Message<SyndEntry> message =
      MessageBuilder.withPayload(entry).build();
    //Send Message on the channel
```

```
    filteredFeedChannel.send(message);
    Message<?> outMessage1 =
      splitFeedOutputChannel.receive(0);
    //Receive Message on channel
    Message<?> outMessage2 =
      splitFeedOutputChannel.receive(0);
    //Assert Results
    assertNotNull("Expected an output message",
      outMessage1);
    assertNotNull("Expected an output message", outMessage2);
    assertThat(outMessage1, hasPayload(category1));
    assertThat(outMessage2, hasPayload(category2));
  }
}
```

This test is pretty self-explanatory. As expected by the original splitter defined in the preceding code, when a payload with SyndEntry having a list of categories is put on the channel, it extracts the list, splits it, and then puts the categories one by one on the output channel.

These are enough samples to get started with Spring Integration testing. The best practices for TDD apply in the context of Spring Integration as well. In fact, apart from the fact that Spring Integration provides support classes for testing the components, there is nothing special about Spring Integration testing.

Summary

We covered how to test most widely used Spring Integration components. It's always good practice to test systems in *isolation* — so that integration time surprises are alleviated to the max. Let's finish our discussion on testing support and move on to the next chapter where we will discuss management and ways to scale up a Spring Integration application.

9

Monitoring, Management, and Scaling Up

In the previous chapter, we covered one of the most important aspects — testing. We will end our discussion on Spring Integration by covering the following topics in this chapter:

- Monitoring and management
- Scaling up

As we have witnessed across the chapters, enterprise systems are disparate, disconnected, and prone to failure. One important aspect of enabling communication across them is the ability to monitor what went wrong, which of the components are overloaded, and what have been the vital stats of communication — this all will help in improving the reliability and efficiency of the systems. The Spring framework provides decent support for monitoring and management, let's discuss how it can be leveraged.

Monitoring and management

There are multiple ways of monitoring and managing operations; for example, the most common way is to use Java's JMX support, another option is to invoke commands remotely, or monitor and log events as they occur — let's cover the most commonly used method.

JMX support

JMX, which is short for **Java Management Extensions**, does not need an introduction—it's a standard way for remote monitoring of applications. Any application can provide implementation of MBeans and then they can be queried to get exposed management information. Spring Integration provides a standard component, which can be used to monitor channels, adapters, and other available components. Standard JMX can be extended to get more specific information.

Prerequisites

Before we can use JMX support from Spring Integration, we need to add namespace declarations and maven dependencies:

- **NameSpace support**: This can be added using the following code snippet:

```
<beans xmlns="http://www.springframework.org/schema/beans"
  xmlns:xsi="http://www.w3.org/2001/XMLSchema-instance"
  xmlns:int="http://www.springframework.org/
    schema/integration"
  xmlns:context="http://www.springframework.org/schema/
    context"
  xmlns:int-jmx="http://www.springframework.org/schema/
    integration/jmx"
  xsi:schemaLocation="http://www.springframework.org/
    schema/integration http://www.springframework.org/
    schema/integration/spring-integration.xsd
    http://www.springframework.org/schema/beans
      http://www.springframework.org/schema/beans/
      spring-beans.xsd
    http://www.springframework.org/schema/context
      http://www.springframework.org/schema/
      context/spring-context.xsd
    http://www.springframework.org/schema/
      integration/jmx http://www.springframework.org/
      schema/integration/jmx/spring-integration-jmx.xsd">
```

- **Maven dependency**: This can be added using the following code snippet:

```
<dependency>
  <groupId>org.springframework.integration</groupId>
  <artifactId>spring-integration-jmx</artifactId>
  <version>${spring.integration.version}</version>
</dependency>
```

- **Initializing the server**: Traditionally, in Java/Spring applications, we need to write code to start the platform MBean server, and export our MBeans, but Spring provides tags to achieve the same tasks. To create and start an MBean server, just use the following line of code:

  ```
  <context:mbean-server/>
  ```

  For exporting the defined MBeans, the following line of code is sufficient:

  ```
  <context:mbean-export/>
  ```

- **Management annotations**: The Spring framework exposes some annotation, which can be used to mark components that will be managed or will help in management and monitoring. For example, `@ManagedResource` indicates a class participating in management and monitoring, while `@ManagedAttribute` and `@ManagedOperation` indicate a member level participation, respectively, for class attribute and operation. Enabling `<context:mbean-export/>` will scan and expose these beans and management nodes. Let's write a sample MBean and export it, we will use this for our examples:

  ```
  import javax.management.Notification;
  import org.springframework.jmx.export.
    annotation.ManagedAttribute;
  import org.springframework.jmx.export.
    annotation.ManagedOperation;
  import org.springframework.jmx.export.
    annotation.ManagedResource;
  import org.springframework.jmx.export.
    notification.NotificationPublisher;
  import org.springframework.jmx.export.
    notification.NotificationPublisherAware;
  import org.springframework.stereotype.Component;

  @Component
  @ManagedResource
  public class TestMBean implements NotificationPublisherAware{
    private NotificationPublisher notificationPublisher;
    private String managedData;

    @ManagedAttribute
    public String getManagedData() {
      return managedData;
    }
    @ManagedAttribute
    public void setManagedData(String managedData) {
      this.managedData = managedData;
    }
  ```

```
@ManagedOperation
public Integer testAdd(Integer num1, Integer num2) {
  notificationPublisher.sendNotification
    (new Notification("testAdd", this, 0));
  return num1 + num2;
}
@Override
public void setNotificationPublisher
  (NotificationPublisher notificationPublisher) {
  this.notificationPublisher = notificationPublisher;
}
}
```

Due to the annotations used, this class will be exported as MBean. Additionally, this class implements `NotificationPublisherAware`, which can be used to send notifications. We will see its usage in the next example.

- **JConsole**: To connect and monitor JMX beans, the easiest way is to use `Jconsole`. It comes bundled with JDK—look for it at `JDK_INSTALLATION_PATH/bin/Jconsole.exe`. By default, JConsole will select a random port, but to have explicit control over the ports of JMX, start the spring integration application with the following parameters:

  ```
  -Dcom.sun.management.jmxremote
  -Dcom.sun.management.jmxremote.port=6969
  -Dcom.sun.management.jmxremote.ssl=false
  -Dcom.sun.management.jmxremote.authenticate=false
  ```

The notification listening channel adapter

The notification listening channel adapter listens for notification sent by MBeans. Any notification received is put on the channel configured. The following code snippet is a sample configuration:

```
<int-jmx:notification-listening-channel-adapter
  id="notifListener"
  channel="listenForNotification"
  object-name="com.cpandey.siexample.jmx:name=testMBean,
  type=TestMBean"/>
```

Let's look at the components used:

- `int-jmx:notification-listening-channel-adapter`: This is the namespace support for the notification listening channel adapter
- `channel`: This is the channel on which the received notification will be put as a message

- `object-name`: This is the name of the MBean, which publishes notifications for this adapter

To test this adapter, follow these steps:

1. Load the configuration context:

```
import org.springframework.context.support.
  AbstractApplicationContext;
import org.springframework.context.support.
  ClassPathXmlApplicationContext;

public final class FeedsExample {
  private FeedsExample() { }

  public static void main(final String... args) {
    final AbstractApplicationContext context =
      new ClassPathXmlApplicationContext
      ("classpath:META-INF/spring/integration/
      spring-integration-context.xml");
  }
}
```

2. Start `Jconsole` and connect to `FeedsExample`.
3. `Jconsole` will list the methods and attributes exposed by `TestMBean`.
4. Invoke add operation, which results in `Testbean` sending a notification.
5. The payload will be put on the `listenForNotification` channel.

Let's write a simple service activator to print the payload:

```
<int:service-activator
  ref="commonServiceActivator"
  method="echoMessageInput"
  input-channel="listenForNotification"/>
```

The notification publishing channel adapter

The notification publishing channel adapter can publish notifications based on data put on the channel. The message put on the channel is used to create notifications. For example, if it is a `String` payload, a `String` type notification will be sent. Here is a sample code snippet:

```
<int:channel id="publishNotification"/>
<int-jmx:notification-publishing-channel-
  adapter id="publishListener"
  channel="publishNotification"
```

```
    object-name="com.cpandey.siexample.
    jmx:name=notificationPublisher"
    default-notification-type="default.notification.type"/>
```

Let's write a small class that can trigger the preceding code snippet:

```java
import org.springframework.context.
  support.AbstractApplicationContext;
import org.springframework.context.
  support.ClassPathXmlApplicationContext;
import org.springframework.integration.support.MessageBuilder;
import org.springframework.messaging.MessageChannel;

public class NotificationPublisher {
  public static void main(String[] args) {
    final AbstractApplicationContext context =
      new ClassPathXmlApplicationContext("classpath:META-
      INF/spring/integration/spring-integration-context.xml");
    try {
      Thread.sleep(60000);
    } catch (InterruptedException e) {
      //do nothing
    }
    MessageChannel publishNotification = context.getBean
      ("publishNotification", MessageChannel.class);
    publishNotification.send(MessageBuilder.withPayload
      ("Sample Message").build());

    MessageChannel triggerOperationChannel = context.getBean
      ("triggerOperationChannel", MessageChannel.class);
    triggerOperationChannel.send(MessageBuilder.
      withPayload("Trigger Method Adapter").build());

    MessageChannel requestOperationChannel = context.getBean
      ("requestOperationChannel", MessageChannel.class);
    requestOperationChannel.send(MessageBuilder.withPayload
      ("Trigger Method Gateway").build());

    MessageChannel input = context.getBean
      ("controlBusChannel", MessageChannel.class);
    String controlMessage =
      "@controlBusTest.controlTestOperation()";
    LOGGER.info("Sending message: " + controlMessage);
    input.send(MessageBuilder.withPayload
      (controlMessage).build());
```

```
    try {
      Thread.sleep(180000);
    } catch (InterruptedException e) {
      //do nothing
    }
    context.stop();
  }
}
```

This is a complete class, which is used to trigger other components described in the following lines of code—the part responsible for triggering the publishing channel adapter is given in the following code snippet:

```
MessageChannel publishNotification = context.
getBean("publishNotification", MessageChannel.class);
    publishNotification.send(MessageBuilder.withPayload
      ("Sample Message").build());
```

The class of the preceding code snippet is pretty simple; it loads the context, gets the reference of a channel, uses the Spring Integration support class `MessageBuilder` to build a payload, and then drops it on the channel. As soon as a message is put on to this channel, an event will be generated and sent across to subscribers. A wait has been introduced to allow some time for `Jconsole` to connect.

The attribute polling channel adapter

As the name suggests, it polls for an attribute that is managed by MBean. The attribute name that needs to be polled and the object name of MBean that encapsulates the attribute are required. The following code is a quick sample configuration of the attribute polling channel adapter:

```
<int:channel id="polledDataChannel"/>
<int-jmx:attribute-polling-channel-adapter id="attribPoller"
  channel="polledDataChannel"
  object-name="com.cpandey.siexample.jmx:name=
  testMBean,type=TestMBean"
  attribute-name="ManagedData">
  <int:poller max-messages-per-poll="1" fixed-rate="5000"/>
</int-jmx:attribute-polling-channel-adapter>
```

The preceding configuration polls the `ManagedData` attribute of `TestMbean`. If the attribute value changes, the changed value is put on the channel. We can have a simple service, given in the following line of code, activate it for testing:

```
<int:service-activator ref="commonServiceActivator"
  method="attributePolled" input-channel="polledDataChannel"/>
```

The tree polling channel adapter

The tree polling channel adapter queries the JMX tree itself and sends a payload, which is the graph of the MBean object. The graph can be further refined using a query—let's write the following sample configuration:

```
<int:channel id="mbeanTreeDataChannel"/>
<int-jmx:tree-polling-channel-adapter  id="treePoller"
  channel="mbeanTreeDataChannel"
  query-name="com.cpandey.siexample.jmx:type=*">
    <int:poller max-messages-per-poll="1" fixed-rate="5000"/>
</int-jmx:tree-polling-channel-adapter>
```

All tags are already covered in the previous example, except query-name—this can be used to restrict the MBean packages. The preceding example code will look for MBeans in the com.cpandey.siexample.jmx package.

We can write a simple service activator to print the MBean graph:

```
<int:service-activator ref="commonServiceActivator"
  method="mbeanTreePolled" input-channel="mbeanTreeDataChannel"/>
```

The operation invoking channel adapter

The operation invoking channel adapter can be used to invoke an operation exposed by MBean, for example setManagedData in TestMbean. Putting a message on the configured channel will trigger the operation and pass the payload as an argument to the invoked operation. The configuration is given in the following code snippet:

```
<int:channel id="triggerOperationChannel"/>
<int-jmx:operation-invoking-channel-adapter
  id="triggerOperation"
  channel="triggerOperationChannel"
  object-name="com.cpandey.siexample.jmx:name=
  testMBean,type=TestMBean"
  operation-name="setManagedData"/>
```

We can use the following code snippet to trigger the preceeding adapter:

```
MessageChannel triggerOperationChannel = context.getBean
  ("triggerOperationChannel", MessageChannel.class);
triggerOperationChannel.send(MessageBuilder.withPayload
  ("Trigger Method Adapter").build());
```

The operation invoking outbound gateway

As usual, `Gateway` is used to make a response available for further processing — in this case, after invoking the operation, a response will be put back on `replychannel` for further processing, as done in the following lines of code:

```
<int:channel id="requestOperationChannel"/>
<int:channel id="replyFromOperationChannel"/>
<int-jmx:operation-invoking-outbound-gateway
    id="triggerOperationGateway"
    request-channel="requestOperationChannel"
    reply-channel="replyFromOperationChannel"
    object-name="com.cpandey.siexample.jmx:name
    =testMBean,type=TestMBean"
    operation-name="getManagedData"/>
```

This code snippet can be triggered using the following lines of code:

```
MessageChannel requestOperationChannel = context.getBean
    ("requestOperationChannel", MessageChannel.class);
requestOperationChannel.send(MessageBuilder.withPayload
    ("Trigger Method Gateway").build());
```

A simple service activator can be plugged in to validate the reslts returned by the gateway.

```
<int:service-activator ref="commonServiceActivator"
  method="operationInvokedGateway" input-channel=
  "replyFromOperationChannel"/>
```

The MBean exporter

What about the standard spring integration components: `MessageChannels`, gateways, and others? Well, they can be exposed for monitoring with the following single line of configuration:

```
<int-jmx:mbean-export
  default-domain="com.cpandey.siexample"
  server="mbeanServer"/>
```

Let's quickly look at the elements used:

* `default-domain`: This is optional and if left blank, `org.springframework.integration` will be used as the default domain

* `server`: This is the reference of `mbeanServer` created using `<context:mbean-server/>`

Before closing the discussion on JMX, let's look at a snapshot of JConsole. Here is the screenshot of the custom MBeans and listeners, which we have exposed:

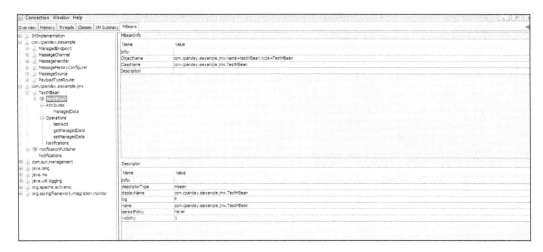

A screenshot showing all the components of Spring Integration, which we have defined in our application, is as follows:

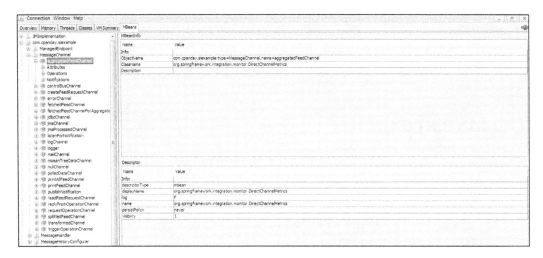

We can observe two aspects:

- The Spring Integration package that lists all spring integration components
- The feeds example that exposes user-defined MBeans

Properties and values of these adapters are pretty self-explanatory, I will leave it to you to explore these further.

Tracking the message

The message flow may throw multiple components—in a typical audit scenario, it may be very helpful to know about all the paths and components the message has been through! Spring Integration provides components to trace the history of a message, just add this snippet in the configuration file:

```
<int:message-history/>
```

Once this is added, all the components through which this message passes (provided that the components have an id tag) have an audit message appended. Let's take the following example:

```
<int:message-history/>

<!-- Notification listening channel adapter -->
<int-jmx:notification-listening-channel-adapter
  id="notifListener"
  channel="listenForNotification"
  object-name="com.cpandey.siexample.jmx:name=
    testMBean,type=TestMBean"/>

<!-- Notification publishing channel adapter -->
<int:channel id="publishNotification"/>
<int-jmx:notification-publishing-channel-adapter
  id="publishListener"
  channel="publishNotification"
  object-name="com.cpandey.siexample.jmx:name=
  notificationPublisher"
  default-notification-type="default.notification.type"/>
```

In this code sample, we have declared `<int:message-history/>` at the start. Also, notice that the next two components `notifListener` and `publishListener` have an ID tag. With this configuration in place, a metadata will be added to the message the moment it passes through these components.

Wire tap

This is extremely simple—it's an interceptor that can be configured with any channel and it will "peek" into all messages going through the channel. This can be used for the purposes of debugging, logging critical information, and so on. Let's add an interceptor to the channel that is listening for the monitoring events:

```
<int:channel id="listenForNotification">
  <int:interceptors>
    <int:wire-tap channel="logger"/>
```

```
    </int:interceptors>
  </int:channel>

<int:logging-channel-adapter
  log-full-message="true" id="logger" level="INFO"/>
```

After adding these configurations, all the messages passing through this channel will be logged.

Control bus

We have elements in spring integration that are being used for application level messaging. How about using the same system to trigger some action? The idea behind control bus is exactly the same—we can define the channel and then, based on the payload on that channel, it can invoke management operations. Let's look at an example:

```
<int:channel id="controlBusChannel"/>
<int:control-bus input-channel="controlBusChannel"/>
```

A class to send a control message to this bus is given in the following lines of code:

```
import org.apache.log4j.Logger;
import org.springframework.jmx.export.annotation.ManagedOperation;
import org.springframework.stereotype.Component;

@Component
public class ControlBusTest {
  private static final Logger LOGGER =
    Logger.getLogger(ControlBusTest.class);
  @ManagedOperation
  public void controlTestOperation() {
    LOGGER.info("controlTestOperation");
  }
}

MessageChannel input = context.getBean
  ("controlBusChannel", MessageChannel.class);
String controlMessage =
  "@controlBusTest.controlTestOperation()";
LOGGER.info("Sending message: " + controlMessage);
input.send(MessageBuilder.withPayload
  (controlMessage).build());
```

With this, let's wrap up our discussion on management and monitoring. In the next section, we will pick one of the most important aspects of application design—scalability.

Scaling up

Scalability of a system is one of the most important non-functional requirements. As we know, there are basically two ways to scale a system: vertical scaling and horizontal scaling. **Vertical scaling** refers to adding more processing power to an existing system—if you are running out of memory, add memory; if CPU cycles are getting short, add some more cores and or make other changes. Not much of a challenge! On the other hand, **horizontal scaling** refers to adding more physical nodes, handling requests in a distributed way, adding redundancy at DB, and message broker components. Obviously, this needs a proper thought-through design. Let's take a couple of ways that can be used to scale Spring applications.

Threading

The most common way to scale a system is to introduce parallel processing. However, before you learn how to do this, let's be aware of the following pitfalls:

- It should be evaluated whether creating a thread will help
- Threads should be created as per machine capability
- We should consider latency across other endpoints
- Threads should be cleaned up

So let's start with an example. We have discussed FTP, if thousands of files are available and we want to process them in parallel, how can this be achieved? We can use `TaskExecutors`, as shown in the following example:

```
<bean id="ftpTaskExecutor" class="org.springframework.scheduling.
  concurrent.ThreadPoolTaskExecutor">
  <property name="maxPoolSize" value="15"/>
  <property name="threadNamePrefix" value="ftpService-"/>
</bean>

<int:service-activator
  ref="ftpFileProcessor"
  method="parserFeedsFromFtp"
  input-channel="ftpInputChannel"
  output-channel="ftpOutputChannel">
    <int:poller fixed-rate="1000"
    receive-timeout="6000"
    task-executor=" ftpTaskExecutor">
  </int:poller>
</int:service-activator>
```

So what is going on in the preceding code? First, we define a task executor — nothing specific to spring integration. You can see that the `org.springframework.scheduling.concurrent.ThreadPoolTaskExecutor` class from the Spring framework is used. Then, we attached this with the poller on the service activator. Now a pool of service will be created, which will process files on the input channel in parallel.

As obvious as it can be, Spring Integration leverages Spring framework's support for executors. The preceding code uses the bean directly, but Spring has provided namespace support as well:

```
<task:executor id="executor"/>
```

The underlying abstraction is `org.springframework.core.task.TaskExecutor`. Whenever a task needs to be executed, it is submitted to the task executor; it is the task executor's job to allocate and de-allocate threads for the task. Let's take the case of the poller from the preceding example, if the elements on the pollable channel are stateless and can be processed concurrently, we can use an executor there:

```
<poller id="defaultPoller" fixed-delay="1000"
   default="true" task-executor="executor"/>
```

If we have a task executor that maintains an underlying pool of threads, then we can specify the maximum threads to be maintained, keeping in view the physical resource limitation:

```
<task:executor id="taskExecutor" pool-size="10"/>
```

Scaling the state

Concurrency will work when there is no state; what about the use cases where we want to scale but at the same time managing the state is mandatory? For example, if the payload is too big, will we wait for all the payloads to be processed, holding the consumers downward? In *Chapter 7, Integration with Spring Batch*, we mentioned that it is possible to trigger the download and then wait for an event that the download has been completed; at that stage, the consumer will kick-in. Similarly, we have some approaches that we can leverage; in fact, we have already covered these in an earlier chapter so I will just touch upon leveraging persistent store for scaling state.

Message store

As the name suggests, we can store the messages temporarily until some criteria is met. For example, if you remember, Aggregator is a spring integration component that correlates and temporarily stores the messages until the completion criteria is satisfied. A similar concept can be used for scaling where the task can be held aside and only processed when all other coordinating members are available. Let's take an example of feeds, some feeds may have pictures associated. The text part will be delivered immediately while the picture delivery may take a lot of time. We can configure aggregator so that it releases the messages when all of the parts have arrived. We already covered how to do this in *Chapter 5, Message Flow*!

Claim check

The concept is very simple, instead of waiting for all the components to arrive, store the part at some known location and have a pointer to it. When the last chunk arrives, "claim" all other parts using the pointer. Obviously, this will apply where we can break the payloads in independent units and the system can be made aware of the final packet arrival. Once implemented, components down the processing chain will get the package only when all of their parts are available — they do not have to wait or be blocked for the duration of complete packet arrival.

Summary

In this chapter, we glanced through monitoring and management aspects of the spring integration framework such as how we can keep an eye on implicit and user-defined integration components, how we can send and receive an event and invoke an operation, and many other aspects. We also covered how threads can be used to scale the application and a couple of ways to scale the state. This brings us to the end of our theoretical journey. In the next chapter; we will write an end-to-end application and finish off our spring integration journey!

10
An End-to-End Example

We have covered enough to get up to speed using Spring Integration in real projects. Let's build a real application, which will exercise different types of components exposed by the Spring Integration module. This will also act as a refresher chapter as we will visit all the concepts discussed so far.

Let's take an example of the feeds aggregator application; it will aggregate feeds based on the configured parameters and then relay it to interested parties. Here is the outline of problems we will try to solve. These are just for the sake of an example, in a real scenario, we might not need the aggregator or splitter, or the sequence of processing itself can be different:

- Ingesting data can be done by:
  ◦ Reading RSS feeds
  ◦ Reading questions from files on an FTP server

- Filtering data:
  ◦ Filtering the valid/invalid messages based on completion criteria; for simplicity, we will filter out `java` questions

- Aggregating messages: Just to showcase the example, we will aggregate and release messages in a group of five

- Splitting a message: The list of aggregated messages will be split and sent down the line for further processing

- Transformation:
  ◦ Converting a message to a format that can be written in DB
  ◦ Converting a message in a JMS format that can be put on a messaging queue
  ◦ Converting a message in an e-mail format so that it can be sent to a subscribed recipient

- Routing a message based on the message type; entity type to database consumer, message type to JMS consumer, and e-mail message to e-mail sender
- Integrating with external systems:
    - ○ Writing to DB
    - ○ Putting on JMS
    - ○ Using an e-mail adapter to send across mails
- JMX: Exposing Spring endpoints for management and monitoring

Prerequisites

Before we can get started with an example, we will need the following software in order to import and run the project:

- A Java IDE (preferably STS, but any other IDE such as Eclipse or NetBeans will also do)
- JDK 1.6 and above
- Maven
- FTP server (this is optional and will only be needed if enabled)

Setting up

Once we have all the prerequisites, follow these steps to launch the program:

1. Check out the project that you've downloaded with the code bundle. It is a Maven project, so using the IDE of your choice, import it as a Maven project.

2. Add settings for the e-mail, JMS, and FTP accounts in `settings.properties`:

```
#URL of RSS feed, as example http://stackoverflow.com/feeds -Make
#sure there are not copyright or legal issues in consumption of
#feed
feeds.url=some valid feed URL
#Username for e-mail account
mail.username=yourusername
#Password for e-mail account
mail.password=yourpassword
#FTP server host
ftp.host=localhost
#FTP port
ftp.port=21
```

```
#Remote directory on FTP which the listener would be observing
ftp.remotefolder=/
#Local directory where downloaded file should be dumped
ftp.localfolder=C:\\Chandan\\Projects\\siexample\\ftp\\
ftplocalfolder
#Username for connecting to FTP server
ftp.username=ftpusername
#Password for connection to FTP server
ftp.password=ftppassword
#JMS broker URL
jms.brolerurl=vm://localhost
```

3. Keep an FTP and an e-mail account ready.

4. Run from the main class, that is, `FeedsExample`.

Ingesting data

Let's start with the first step, ingestion of data. We have configured two data sources: RSS feeds and an FTP server, let's take a look at these.

Ingesting data from the RSS feed

The following code snippet is the configuration for a feed adapter; this fetches feed from the configured `url` and puts it on the channel:

```
<int-feed:inbound-channel-adapter
  id="soJavaFeedAdapterForAggregator"
  channel="fetchedFeedChannel"
  auto-startup="true"
  url="${feeds.url}">
  <int:poller
    fixed-rate="500" max-messages-per-poll="1" />
</int-feed:inbound-channel-adapter>
```

 I will show the code and explain what it does, but will not cover each and every tag in detail as they have already been covered in the respective chapters.

Ingesting data from an FTP server

Now, for this to work, you need an FTP server configured. For testing, you can always set up an FTP server locally. Depending on your FTP server location and configuration parameters, set up a session factory:

```
<!-- FTP Create Session-->
  <bean id="ftpClientSessionFactory"
    class="org.springframework.integration.
    ftp.session.DefaultFtpSessionFactory">
    <property name="host" value="${ftp.host}"/>
    <property name="port" value="${ftp.port}"/>
    <property name="username" value="${ftp.username}"/>
    <property name="password" value="${ftp.password}"/>
  </bean>
```

After we have set up the session factory, it can be used to establish a connection with the FTP server. The following code will download the new file from the configured `remote-directory` of the FTP and put it in the `local-directory`:

```
<!-- FTP Download files from server and put it in local directory-
  -->
  <int-ftp:inbound-channel-adapter
    channel="fetchedFeedChannel"
    session-factory="ftpClientSessionFactory"
    remote-directory="${ftp.remotefolder}"
    local-directory="${ftp.localfolder}"
    auto-create-local-directory="true"
    delete-remote-files="true"
    filename-pattern="*.txt"
    local-filename-generator-expression="#this.toLowerCase() +
    '.trns'">
    <int:poller fixed-rate="1000"/>
  </int-ftp:inbound-channel-adapter>
```

Filtering the data

The feed and FTP adapter fetch the feed and put it on to `fetchedFeedChannel`. Let's configure a filter, which will allow only Java-related questions, while reading the feeds. It will read feeds from the channel `fetchedFeedChannel` and pass on the filtered feeds to the channel `fetchedFeedChannelForAggregatior`. The following code snippet is the Spring configuration:

```
<bean id="filterSoFeedBean" class=
  "com.cpandey.siexample.filter.SoFeedFilter"/>
<!--Filter the feed which are not for Java category -->
```

```
<int:filter
   input-channel="fetchedFeedChannel"
   output-channel="fetchedFeedChannelForAggregatior"
   ref="filterSoFeedBean"
   method="filterFeed"/>
```

Here is the JavaBean class encapsulating the logic of the filter:

```java
import java.util.List;
import org.apache.log4j.Logger;
import org.springframework.messaging.Message;
import com.sun.syndication.feed.synd.SyndCategoryImpl;
import com.sun.syndication.feed.synd.SyndEntry;

public class SoFeedFilter {
   private static final Logger LOGGER =
      Logger.getLogger(SoFeedFilter.class);
   public boolean filterFeed(Message<SyndEntry> message){
      SyndEntry entry = message.getPayload();
      List<SyndCategoryImpl> categories=entry.getCategories();
      if(categories!=null&&categories.size()>0){
         for (SyndCategoryImpl category: categories) {
            if(category.getName().equalsIgnoreCase("java")){
               LOGGER.info("JAVA category feed");
               return true;
            }
         }
      }
      return false;
   }
}
```

The aggregator

The aggregator is for showcasing the aggregator usage. An aggregator is plugged on the output channel of the filter, that is, fetchedFeedChannelForAggregatior. We will use all the three components of aggregator: correlation, completion, and aggregator. Let's declare the beans:

```
<bean id="soFeedCorrelationStrategyBean"
   class="com.cpandey.siexample.aggregator.CorrelationStrategy"/>

<bean id="sofeedCompletionStrategyBean"
   class="com.cpandey.siexample.aggregator.CompletionStrategy"/>

<bean id="aggregatorSoFeedBean"
   class="com.cpandey.siexample.aggregator.SoFeedAggregator"/>
```

Once we have defined the three vital components of an aggregator, let's define the component, which will aggregate feeds in a group of five and then release only on the next channel:

```
<int:aggregator input-channel="fetchedFeedChannelForAggregatior"
  output-channel="aggregatedFeedChannel"
    ref="aggregatorSoFeedBean"
  method="aggregateAndPublish" release-strategy=
    "sofeedCompletionStrategyBean"
  release-strategy-method="checkCompleteness" correlation-
    strategy="soFeedCorrelationStrategyBean"
  correlation-strategy-method="groupFeedsBasedOnCategory"
  message-store="messageStore" expire-groups-upon-completion="true">
  <int:poller fixed-rate="1000"></int:poller>
</int:aggregator>
```

The correlation bean

If you remember, the correlation bean holds the strategy to group "related" items. We will simply use the category of feeds to group messages:

```
import java.util.List;
import org.apache.log4j.Logger;
import org.springframework.messaging.Message;
import com.sun.syndication.feed.synd.SyndCategoryImpl;
import com.sun.syndication.feed.synd.SyndEntry;

public class CorrelationStrategy {
  private static final Logger LOGGER = Logger.
getLogger(CorrelationStrategy.class);

  //aggregator's method should expect a Message<?> and return an
  //Object.
  public Object groupFeedsBasedOnCategory(Message<?> message) {
    //Which messages will be grouped in a bucket
    //-say based on category, based on some ID etc.
    if(message!=null){
      SyndEntry entry = (SyndEntry)message.getPayload();
      List<SyndCategoryImpl> categories=entry.getCategories();
      if(categories!=null&&categories.size()>0){
        for (SyndCategoryImpl category: categories) {
          //for simplicity, lets consider the first category
          LOGGER.info("category "+category.getName());
          return category.getName();
        }
      }
```

```
        }
      return null;
    }
  }
```

The completion bean

We have correlated the messages, but for how long will we hold on to the list? This will will be decided by the completion criteria. Let's put a very simple criteria that if there are five feeds from the same category, then release it for further processing. Here is the class implementing this:

```java
import java.util.List;
import org.apache.log4j.Logger;
import com.sun.syndication.feed.synd.SyndEntry;

public class CompletionStrategy {
  private static final Logger LOGGER =
    Logger.getLogger(CompletionStrategy.class);
  //Completion strategy is used by aggregator to decide whether all
  //components has
  //been aggregated or not method should expect a java.util.List
  //Object returning a Boolean value
  public boolean checkCompleteness(List<SyndEntry> messages) {
    if(messages!=null){
      if(messages.size()>4){
        LOGGER.info("All components assembled, releasing
          aggregated message");
        return true;
      }
    }
    return false;
  }

}
```

The aggregator bean

Feeds will be correlated and, after the completion criteria is satisfied, the aggregator will return the list on the next endpoint. We have already defined the correlation strategy and completion criteria earlier, let's see the code for the aggregator:

```java
import java.util.List;
import org.apache.log4j.Logger;
import com.sun.syndication.feed.synd.SyndEntry;
```

```
public class SoFeedAggregator {
  private static final Logger LOGGER =
    Logger.getLogger(SoFeedAggregator.class);
  public List<SyndEntry> aggregateAndPublish
    ( List<SyndEntry> messages) {
    LOGGER.info("SoFeedAggregator -Aggregation complete");
    return messages;
  }
}
```

The splitter

The aggregator will aggregate the message and put it on the `aggregatedFeedChannel`. Let's have a splitter wired on this channel, which can split back the list of messages and pass one at a time for further processing on to the `splittedFeedChannel` channel. The Spring configuration is given in the following code snippet:

```
<int:splitter
  ref="splitterSoFeedBean"
  method="splitAndPublish"
  input-channel="aggregatedFeedChannel"
  output-channel="splittedFeedChannel" />
```

The JavaBean with the splitter logic:

```
import java.util.List;
import com.sun.syndication.feed.synd.SyndEntry;
public class SoFeedSplitter {
  public List<SyndEntry> splitAndPublish(List<SyndEntry> message) {
    //Return one message from list at a time -this will be picked up
    //by the processor
    return message;
  }
}
```

Transformation

Now that we have feeds in the RSS format, let's transform it to appropriate formats so that the endpoints responsible for persisting in the database, putting it on the JMS channel, and sending it as a mail, can understand that. The splitter will put one message at a time on the channel `splittedFeedChannel`. Let's declare this as a pub-sub channel and attach three endpoints, which will be our transformers. Configure the pub-sub channel as follows:

```
<int:publish-subscribe-channel id="splittedFeedChannel"/>
```

The configuration for the three transformers that we have used is as follows:

```
<bean id="feedDbTransformerBean" class=
  "com.cpandey.siexample.transformer.SoFeedDbTransformer" />

<bean id="feedJMSTransformerBean" class=
  "com.cpandey.siexample.transformer.SoFeedJMSTransformer" />

<bean id="feedMailTransformerBean" class=
  "com.cpandey.siexample.transformer.SoFeedMailTransformer" />
```

The DB transformer

Let's write the transformer component from the Spring Integration and Java class that have the transformation logic:

```
<int:transformer id="dbFeedTransformer" ref=
  "feedDbTransformerBean"
  input-channel="splittedFeedChannel"
  method="transformFeed"
  output-channel="transformedChannel"/>

import org.apache.log4j.Logger;
import org.springframework.messaging.Message;
import com.cpandey.siexample.pojo.SoFeed;
import com.sun.syndication.feed.synd.SyndEntry;

public class SoFeedDbTransformer {
  private static final Logger LOGGER =
    Logger.getLogger(SoFeedDbTransformer.class);

  public SoFeed transformFeed(Message<SyndEntry> message){
    SyndEntry entry = message.getPayload();
    SoFeed soFeed=new SoFeed();
    soFeed.setTitle(entry.getTitle());
    soFeed.setDescription(entry.getDescription().getValue());
    soFeed.setCategories(entry.getCategories());
    soFeed.setLink(entry.getLink());
    soFeed.setAuthor(entry.getAuthor());
    LOGGER.info("JDBC :: "+soFeed.getTitle());
    return soFeed;
  }
}
```

The JMS transformer

Here is the code for the JMS transformer component declaration and the corresponding JavaBean:

```
<int:transformer id="jmsFeedTransformer" ref="feedJMSTransformerBean"
  input-channel="splittedFeedChannel"
  method="transformFeed"
  output-channel="transformedChannel"/>
```

```java
import org.apache.log4j.Logger;
import org.springframework.messaging.Message;
import com.cpandey.siexample.pojo.SoFeed;
import com.sun.syndication.feed.synd.SyndEntry;
public class SoFeedJMSTransformer {
  private static final Logger LOGGER =
    Logger.getLogger(SoFeedJMSTransformer.class);

  public String transformFeed(Message<SyndEntry> message){
    SyndEntry entry = message.getPayload();
    SoFeed soFeed=new SoFeed();
    soFeed.setTitle(entry.getTitle());
    soFeed.setDescription(entry.getDescription().getValue());
    soFeed.setCategories(entry.getCategories());
    soFeed.setLink(entry.getLink());
    soFeed.setAuthor(entry.getAuthor());
    //For JSM , return String
    LOGGER.info("JMS"+soFeed.getTitle());
    return soFeed.toString();
  }
}
```

The mail transformer

Finally, let's write the configuration and code for the mail transformer:

```
<int:transformer id="mailFeedTransformer"
  ref="feedMailTransformerBean"
  input-channel="splittedFeedChannel"
  method="transformFeed"
  output-channel="transformedChannel"/>
```

```java
import java.util.Date;
import org.apache.log4j.Logger;
import org.springframework.mail.MailMessage;
import org.springframework.mail.SimpleMailMessage;
import org.springframework.messaging.Message;
```

```
import com.cpandey.siexample.pojo.SoFeed;
import com.sun.syndication.feed.synd.SyndEntry;

public class SoFeedMailTransformer {
  private static final Logger LOGGER =
    Logger.getLogger(SoFeedMailTransformer.class);

  public MailMessage transformFeed(Message<SyndEntry> message){
    SyndEntry entry = message.getPayload();
    SoFeed soFeed=new SoFeed();
    soFeed.setTitle(entry.getTitle());
    soFeed.setDescription(entry.getDescription().getValue());
    soFeed.setCategories(entry.getCategories());
    soFeed.setLink(entry.getLink());
    soFeed.setAuthor(entry.getAuthor());

    //For Mail return MailMessage
    MailMessage msg = new SimpleMailMessage();
    msg.setTo("emailaddress");
    msg.setFrom("emailaddress");
    msg.setSubject("Subject");
    msg.setSentDate(new Date());
    msg.setText("Mail Text");
    LOGGER.info("Mail Message"+soFeed.getTitle());

      return msg;
  }
}
```

Router

After transforming the messages to appropriate formats, the transformers put the message on to the channel transformedChannel. We have three type of messages that will be processed by different endpoints. We can use the payload router that will route it to different components based on the payload type:

```
<int:payload-type-router input-channel="transformedChannel"
  default-output-channel="logChannel">
<int:mapping type="com.cpandey.siexample.pojo.SoFeed"
  channel="jdbcChannel" />
<int:mapping type="java.lang.String"
  channel="jmsChannel" />
<int:mapping type="org.springframework.mail.MailMessage"
  channel="mailChannel" />
</int:payload-type-router>
```

Integration

Now is the time for actual integration! Once the router has routed the message to the appropriate endpoints, it should be processed by them. For example, it can be persisted to a database, sent on a JMS channel, or sent as an e-mail. Depending on the payload type, the router will put the message on to one of the channels `jdbcChannel`, `jmsChannel`, or `mailChannel`. If it cannot understand the payload, it will route it to `logChannel`. Let's start with the endpoint attached to the channel `jdbcChannel` that is used for database integration.

Database integration

In this section, we will write code to add and query data from a database. Before we write adapters from Spring Integration, let's do the basic setup.

Prerequisites

As obvious as it can be, we need a database where we can dump the data. For simplicity, we will use the in-memory database. Let's also configure the ORM provider, transaction, and other aspects to be used with the database:

- Declaration of the embedded database:

```
<jdbc:embedded-database id="dataSource" type="H2"/>
```

- Declaration of the transaction manager:

```
<bean id="transactionManager" class=
  "org.springframework.orm.jpa.JpaTransactionManager">
  <constructor-arg ref="entityManagerFactory" />
</bean>
```

- Declaration of the entity manager factory:

```
<bean id="entityManagerFactory"
  class="org.springframework.orm.jpa.
    LocalContainerEntityManagerFactoryBean">
  <property name="dataSource"  ref="dataSource" />
  <property name="jpaVendorAdapter"
    ref="vendorAdaptor" />
  <property name="packagesToScan"
    value="com.cpandey.siexample.pojo"/>
</bean>
```

- Declaration of the entity manager:

```
<bean id="entityManager" class="org.springframework.orm.
  jpa.support.SharedEntityManagerBean">
```

```
      <property name="entityManagerFactory"
        ref="entityManagerFactory"/>
    </bean>
```

- Declaration of the abstract vendor adapter:

```
<bean id="abstractVendorAdapter" abstract="true">
  <property name="generateDdl" value="true" />
  <property name="database"    value="H2" />
  <property name="showSql"     value="false"/>
</bean>
```

- Declaration of the actual vendor adapter, in our case, it is hibernate:

```
<bean id="vendorAdaptor" class="org.springframework.orm.
  jpa.vendor.HibernateJpaVendorAdapter"
  parent="abstractVendorAdaptor">
</bean>
```

The gateway

Let's define a gateway, which will insert invoke methods to insert feeds and then read them back from the database:

```
<int:gateway id="feedService"
  service-interface="com.cpandey.siexample.service.FeedService"
  default-request-timeout="5000"
  default-reply-timeout="5000">
  <int:method name="createFeed"
    request-channel="createFeedRequestChannel"/>
  <int:method name="readAllFeed"
    reply-channel="readFeedRequestChannel"/>
</int:gateway>
```

The bean definition for the gateway is as follows:

```
import java.util.List;
import com.cpandey.siexample.pojo.FeedEntity;
public interface FeedService {
  FeedEntity createFeed(FeedEntity feed);
  List<FeedEntity> readAllFeed();
}
```

The service activator

This service activator is plugged in to the `jdbcChannel` channel. When a message arrives, its `persistFeedToDb` method is invoked, which uses the preceding gateway to persist the feeds:

```java
import org.apache.log4j.Logger;
import org.springframework.beans.factory.annotation.Autowired;
import org.springframework.integration.annotation.MessageEndpoint;
import org.springframework.integration.annotation.ServiceActivator;
import com.cpandey.siexample.pojo.FeedEntity;
import com.cpandey.siexample.pojo.SoFeed;

@MessageEndpoint
public class PersistFeed {

  private static final Logger LOGGER =
    Logger.getLogger(PersistFeed.class);

  @Autowired FeedService feedService;
  @ServiceActivator
  public void persistFeedToDb(SoFeed feed) {
    //This will write to output channel of gateway
    //From there this will be picked by updating adapter
    feedService.createFeed(new FeedEntity(feed.getTitle()));
  }

  @ServiceActivator
  public void printFeed(FeedEntity feed) {
    //Print the feed fetched by retrieving adapter
    LOGGER.info("Feed Id"+feed.getId()+" Feed Title "
      +feed.getTitle());
  }
}
```

Gateways for updating and reading the feeds

Finally, we plug in the Spring Integration updating and retrieving outbound gateways to persist and read back the feed:

```xml
<int-jpa:updating-outbound-gateway
  entity-manager-factory="entityManagerFactory"
  request-channel="createFeedRequestChannel"
  entity-class="com.cpandey.siexample.pojo.FeedEntity"
  reply-channel="printAllFeedChannel">
```

```
<int-jpa:transactional transaction-manager=
    "transactionManager" />
</int-jpa:updating-outbound-gateway>

<int-jpa:retrieving-outbound-gateway
    entity-manager-factory="entityManagerFactory"
    request-channel="readFeedRequestChannel"
    jpa-query="select f from FeedEntity f order by f.title asc"
    reply-channel="printAllFeedChannel">
</int-jpa:retrieving-outbound-gateway>
```

Sending a mail

We can use the Spring Integration mail outbound channel adapter to send out mails. It needs a reference to the mail sender class, which has been configured as follows:

- Spring Integration component for sending mail:

```
<int-mail:outbound-channel-adapter
    channel="mailChannel"
    mail-sender="mailSender"/>
```

As evident in the preceding configuration, this adapter is plugged in to mailChannel—one of the other channels where the router routes the message.

- The mail sender used by the preceding component:

```
<bean id="mailSender"
    class="org.springframework.mail.
    javamail.JavaMailSenderImpl">
    <property name="javaMailProperties">
      <props>
        <prop key="mail.smtp.auth">true</prop>
        <prop key="mail.smtp.starttls.enable">true</prop>
        <prop key="mail.smtp.host">smtp.gmail.com</prop>
        <prop key="mail.smtp.port">587</prop>
      </props>
    </property>
    <property name="username" value="${mail.username}" />
    <property name="password" value="${mail.password}" />
</bean>
```

Putting messages on to the JMS queue

Finally, let's use the outbound channel adapter to put the message on to a JMS queue, this polls the channel `jmsChannel` for a message and whenever router routes a message here, it puts it on to the `destination` queue:

```
<int-jms:outbound-channel-adapter
  connection-factory="connectionFactory"
  channel="jmsChannel"
  destination="feedInputQueue" />
```

To test the message on the queue, let's plug in a simple service activator:

```
<int:service-activator
  ref="commonServiceActivator"
  method="echoJmsMessageInput"
  input-channel="jmsProcessedChannel"/>
```

As evident in the preceding configuration, we need `destination` and `connection-factory`, let's configure these:

```
<bean id="feedInputQueue" class=
  "org.apache.activemq.command.ActiveMQQueue">
  <constructor-arg value="queue.input"/>
</bean>

<bean id="connectionFactory"
  class="org.springframework.jms.connection.
  CachingConnectionFactory">
  <property name="targetConnectionFactory">
    <bean class="org.apache.activemq.ActiveMQConnectionFactory">
      <property name="brokerURL"
        value="${jms.brokerurl}"/>
    </bean>
  </property>
  <property name="sessionCacheSize" value="10"/>
  <property name="cacheProducers" value="false"/>
</bean>
```

Exporting as an MBean

Finally, let's add code to export the components used as MBeans, which can be monitored through JConsole or other JMX tools:

```
<int-jmx:mbean-export
  default-domain="com.cpandey.siexample"
  server="mbeanServer"/>
```

Summary

We covered an end-to-end example in this chapter; I hope this was useful and served the purpose of refreshing the concept and a complete use case in one place. With this, our Spring Integration journey has ended. I hope you enjoyed it!

We covered most common features of the Spring Integration framework and introduced enough material to gain momentum. If this book excites you about using Spring Integration, the official reference available at `http://docs.spring.io/ spring-integration/reference/htmlsingle` should be your next stop.

Index

Thank you for buying
Spring Integration Essentials

About Packt Publishing

Packt, pronounced 'packed', published its first book, *Mastering phpMyAdmin for Effective MySQL Management*, in April 2004, and subsequently continued to specialize in publishing highly focused books on specific technologies and solutions.

Our books and publications share the experiences of your fellow IT professionals in adapting and customizing today's systems, applications, and frameworks. Our solution-based books give you the knowledge and power to customize the software and technologies you're using to get the job done. Packt books are more specific and less general than the IT books you have seen in the past. Our unique business model allows us to bring you more focused information, giving you more of what you need to know, and less of what you don't.

Packt is a modern yet unique publishing company that focuses on producing quality, cutting-edge books for communities of developers, administrators, and newbies alike. For more information, please visit our website at www.packtpub.com.

About Packt Open Source

In 2010, Packt launched two new brands, Packt Open Source and Packt Enterprise, in order to continue its focus on specialization. This book is part of the Packt Open Source brand, home to books published on software built around open source licenses, and offering information to anybody from advanced developers to budding web designers. The Open Source brand also runs Packt's Open Source Royalty Scheme, by which Packt gives a royalty to each open source project about whose software a book is sold.

Writing for Packt

We welcome all inquiries from people who are interested in authoring. Book proposals should be sent to author@packtpub.com. If your book idea is still at an early stage and you would like to discuss it first before writing a formal book proposal, then please contact us; one of our commissioning editors will get in touch with you.

We're not just looking for published authors; if you have strong technical skills but no writing experience, our experienced editors can help you develop a writing career, or simply get some additional reward for your expertise.

Spring MVC Beginner's Guide

ISBN: 978-1-78328-487-0   Paperback: 304 pages

Your ultimate guide to building a complete web application using all the capabilities of Spring MVC

1. Carefully crafted exercises, with detailed explanations for each step, to help you understand the concepts with ease.

2. You will gain a clear understanding of the end to end request/response life cycle, and each logical component's responsibility.

3. Packed with tips and tricks that will demonstrate the industry best practices on developing a Spring-MVC-based application.

Instant Spring Tool Suite

ISBN: 978-1-78216-414-2   Paperback: 76 pages

A practical guide for kick-starting your Spring projects using the Spring Tool Suite IDE

1. Learn something new in an Instant! A short, fast, focused guide delivering immediate results.

2. Learn how to use Spring Tool Suite to jump-start your Spring projects.

3. Develop, test, and deploy your applications, all within the IDE.

4. Simple, step-by-step instructions in an easy-to-follow format.

Spring Security 3.x Cookbook

ISBN: 978-1-78216-752-5   Paperback: 300 pages

Over 60 recipes to help you successfully safeguard your web applications with Spring Security

1. Learn about all the mandatory security measures for modern day applications using Spring Security.

2. Investigate different approaches to application level authentication and authorization.

3. Master how to mount security on applications used by developers and organizations.

Spring Web Flow 2 Web Development

ISBN: 978-1-84719-542-5   Paperback: 200 pages

Master Spring's well-designed web frameworks to develop powerful web applications

1. Design, develop, and test your web applications using the Spring Web Flow 2 framework.

2. Enhance your web applications with progressive AJAX, Spring security integration, and Spring Faces.

3. Stay up-to-date with the latest version of Spring Web Flow.

4. Walk through the creation of a bug tracker web application with clear explanations.

Please check **www.PacktPub.com** for information on our titles